S

Everybody's Guide to the Magical World of QR Codes

Barcodes, Mobile Devices and Hyperlinking the Real to the Virtual

Mick Winter

Westsong Publishing

Napa, California

www.westsongpublishing.com

Scan Me

Everybody's Guide to the Magical World of QR Codes

Barcodes, Mobile Devices and
Hyperlinking the Real to the Virtual

Copyright © 2010 by Mick Winter

Published by
Westsong Publishing
Napa CA 94558
www.westsongpublishing.com

First print edition published 2011
ISBN 978-0-9659000-3-4

Library of Congress Control Number: 2010938357

Printed in the United States of America

Dedication

To Denso-Wave for inventing QR codes and making them available to everyone, to Tim Berners-Lee for inventing the World Wide Web, and to Tara Brabazon, for a great Master's program.

Acknowledgments

QR Code is a registered trademark of DENSO WAVE INC.

Special thanks to JO Bugental for his invaluable editing, and to Nancy Shapiro for another of her always exceptional book covers.

Visit Us Online

www.scanmebook.com

Table of Contents

Quick Shortcuts

If you want to know what a *QR Code* is, go to page 17.

If you want to know about *other kinds of barcodes*, go to page 105.

If you want to get a *reader* for your mobile phone so you can scan QR Codes, go to page 23.

If you want to use your phone for *comparative shopping*, go to page 108.

If you want to make *your own QR Codes*, go to page 27.

If you want to know how to use QR Codes with S*ocial Media*, go to page 92.

If you want to know about making *Mobile Websites*, go to page 41.

If you want to know about QR Codes and E*ducation*, go to page 129.

If you want to know how to use QR Codes for your particular *business, activity or interest*, start at page 50.

If you want to know about QR Code *history and specifications*, go to page 117.

If you want to know about *academic research* into barcodes, go to page 129.

Introduction

Imagine you could take your mobile phone, hold it up to an image, and magically be transported to any information you wished. It would be like having a genie of the lamp without the subservient insolence.

Suppose you see a movie poster and wonder if the movie is worth seeing. Zap! You're watching the movie's trailer. You look at a menu in a restaurant's front window and wonder if the food is as good as it looks. Zap! You're reading reviews from people who tell you first hand how they liked the restaurant.

Suppose you're reading a newspaper article and would like to know more about the article's subject. Zap! You're reading a different article, or seeing a news video, or hearing a radio interview about the same subject. Imagine you're at a subway stop and wondering when the next train will come. Zap! You're looking at the schedule and also finding out if the train's on time.

If you lived in Japan, you wouldn't have to imagine or suppose. It's been happening for years. Same in South Korea. Now it's happening in Europe, and just beginning in the U.S. and Canada.

How does this magic happen? With something called a QR (Quick Response) Code. *This* is a QR Code:

I became interested in QR codes[1] a couple of years ago. At the time, I became convinced that QR codes would become immensely popular in the United States. Some time ago I started putting QR codes on my business cards, so that someone merely had to scan the code and all of my contact information would immediately be entered into their mobile phone's address book.

Then, in the spring of 2010, I conducted a research project with QR codes where I live—in California's Napa Valley. The purpose of my research project was to determine—and increase—awareness and use of QR codes in the Napa Valley. In the early stages of the project, as I was establishing sites

---

1   QR Code is a registered trademark of DENSO WAVE INCORPORATED.

where QR codes could be displayed, I discovered that almost no one had ever seen them before. When I explained what QR codes were, some people immediately started seeing possibilities and began to come up with ideas for their particular business that went beyond those I had suggested. However, others said, upon hearing about QR codes and seeing a demonstration, "That's interesting. But how can we use them in our business? Can we make money with them?"

Considering that we were in the midst of an economic depression, it was a legitimate question. I started thinking of specific ideas I could give them on how they could be used. I decided to go to Amazon, pick a book on QR codes that I could probably recommend after reading, and order it.

There wasn't one. Not only was there not a *good* book, there wasn't *any* book.

There is now.

Enjoy. I hope you find it useful.

...oh, and one other thing. The world of QR codes is so dynamic that I'm sure *you've* got ideas on how this book could be improved and expanded. If so, email me at **mick@westsong.com**. I'd like to hear your ideas.

Mick Winter

About QR Codes

What is a QR code?

So now you have a book in your hands (or perhaps on your ebook reader) about QR codes. Fine, you say. Thanks for the book. But what *are* they?

Here again is what one looks like.

To help you understand what a QR code *is*, here's what a QR code *doesn't* look like:

This smaller code with numbers below it is a standard *barcode*. You've seen them everywhere on products and books. Manufacturers, distributors, shippers and retail sellers use them to keep track of inventory. If you scan the barcode above, you'll see information on a book. The numbers "9 780965 900058" make up the book's *ISBN number*, which is used on a type of barcode (EAN-13) that is a universal standard for identifying book titles. It happens to be for a book I wrote titled "Sustainable Living for Home, Neighborhood and Community".

Although there are websites where you can generate an ISBN barcode at no charge, we always prefer to spend $10 and get one that we know we can count on. We recommend: http://www.createbarcodes.com

A barcode is one-dimensional. In other words, the scanner scans the code in only one direction: horizontally. The height really doesn't matter. The information remains the same no matter how tall the image is. Because a barcode is one-dimensional, it contains a relatively limited amount of information, usually no more than 20 characters, and generally less. Yes, it could contain more data if you kept stretching the barcode, making it wider and wider. But there are limits to the space available on a package or book, as well as limits on the viewing field of your scanner. So, QR codes were invented.

A QR code is *two*-dimensional, meaning that the information changes vertically as well as horizontally. A QR code reader scans *up* as well as *across*. This enables a QR code to contain much more information than a barcode. It also requires a more sophisticated reader, but you don't have to worry about that. That's already been taken care of by software and hardware engineers. You can download—at no charge—a number of very sophisticated QR code readers for your mobile phone.

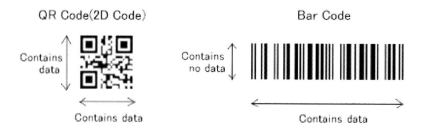

QR codes were invented in Japan in 1994 by Denso Wave[2], a subsidiary of Toyota. "QR" means "Quick Response". Denso wanted a code that could be *de*coded very quickly in order to keep track of a very large number of items in their inventory. While the term "QR code" remains a registered trademark of Denso Wave Incorporated, and Denso retains the patent on QR code technology, it has released all of the information on creating and scanning them so that they can be used by people all over the world at no charge and with no obligation to Denso. You need no license to create or use QR codes. It was a very generous act—and one from which you can benefit.

---

2 http://www.denso-wave.com/qrcode/aboutqr-e.html

Why should I scan QR codes?

QR Codes are:

- **Fun**

  QR codes are new and unique. Plus there's almost something magical about them because that can instantly connect you to a virtual universe of information and entertainment.

- **Convenient and Fast**

  All it takes is a fast and easy scan with your camera's phone—which most of us, of all ages, carry with us.

- **Useful**

  QR codes can send information to your mobile phone immediately, whatever your location.

Why should my business use QR codes?

- **They're free.**

  Although you can find companies that will charge you to create them, you can easily do it yourself at no charge.

- **They give you fast feedback on your marketing.**

  You can track each time one of your QR codes is scanned, using free or paid services. You'll know soon and thoroughly just how well your print, TV, digital and other advertising media are working. (You'll learn more about *tracking* later in this book.)

- **Customers—and potential customers—respond to them.**

  Initially they're a novelty, later they're a necessity. People scan them because they're fun and useful. They like interacting with your message and getting or learning something they couldn't get otherwise.

- **They make your life easier**

  Using QR codes in combination with customer support—for example to connect with user manuals and troubleshooting information—saves you staff, time and money.

Not surprisingly, since they were invented in Japan, that country is the biggest user of QR codes. One study several years ago showed that 80 percent of the Japanese population had used QR codes within the past two weeks. But even that doesn't indicate the true popularity of QR codes in Japan.

Almost all mobile phones in Japan can read QR codes and South Korea is very similar. Europe is catching up; the United States is relatively new to the game, but active, thanks to the iPhone, Google's Android operation system, and Windows Mobile phones, as well as Finnish manufacturer Nokia's phones. In fact, almost all new phones in the US, except for those designed for people who specifically don't want this feature, offer Internet access and a camera and therefore the ability to scan and decode QR codes.

A QR code can contain up to 4,296 characters of information. This is adequate for many purposes, but insufficient for many others. Fortunately there's a solution to this limit. Thanks to the invention of the World Wide Web (Thanks, Sir Tim[3]) a QR code can serve as a digital doorway to the vast, literally infinite, information on the Web. By placing a web address (known formally as a URL – Uniform Resource Locator) in the QR code, a barcode reader can lead your mobile phone to a webpage on the Internet, and from there to anywhere else that's relevant on the Web. Thanks to two important inventions, the World Wide Web and QR codes, you now have the tools you need to have fun *and* make a profit.

The digital connection between the QR code that you scan and the information on the web that you can read (or see or hear) is a form of "hyperlink". Ordinarily, a *hyperlink* is a link on a webpage that links to another webpage. You'll often see it underlined, in a different color, or somehow otherwise marked so that it stands out from the rest of the text. Both the link on the webpage and the webpage to which it links are *digital*; that is, they're made up of electronic bits and bytes. When you scan an object, whether it's a magazine, a sign, a cereal box or a poster, that object is real. It's "hard". So the link provided by a QR code between the "real" object and the "virtual" information, is sometimes referred to as a "hardlink". It can also be called a "physical world hyperlink". Whatever it's called, it *links*. And that link opens up the world to you through your mobile phone.

3 Tim Berners-Lee invented the World Wide Web while working at CERN Laboratory in Switzerland in 1989. In 2004, he was knighted by British Queen Elizabeth.

How are QR codes already being used?

Using QR codes is an act of *object hyperlinking*, or *physical world linking*. The codes are your link between the physical world and the virtual world. Using a special but easily and freely available software application, you use your phone's camera to scan a real-world object (sign, product, piece of paper, newspaper, television screen) and you're immediately connected to information about, or connected with, that object. It's as if the information is hidden in the object, and the magic viewer (your phone) reveals that hidden information to you.

QR codes have come a long way since their initial use tracking auto parts. We'll go into much more detail later in this book in our **A to Z section**, but briefly a QR code can provide, or lead to, the following—and much more:

> **Product information**, including price, country of origin[4], countries it has passed through since it was manufactured, energy use in operation and in its manufacture, users manual, warranty, service locations, troubleshooting, safety warnings.

> **Food products**: Agricultural information including location grown, comments from the grower, processing locations, lot number, ingredients if a processed product, price, nutritional information, organic/natural food status, recipes, packaging date, sell by date, allergic products information.

> **Transportation**: Train, bus, subway, tram, plane, ferry schedules, car and foot navigation.

> **Entertainment**: Showtimes, locations, prices, content, reviews, paperless tickets, new release and pre-release songs.

> **Vending machines**: Food, beverage and gadget purchases, DVD rental.

> **Business cards**: Name, company, position, address, phones, email, websites, comments.

> **DVDs/CDs**: Photos, videos, music tracks, reviews, where to purchase similar albums or films, information on musicians and actors.

---

4   List of Country Codes - Country codes are a standard of GS1, an international not-for-profit association dedicated to the development and implementation of global standards. To see the codes, go to
    http://en.wikipedia.org/wiki/List_of_GS1_country_codes

Retail businesses: Website, reviews such as Yelp and Google Places, discount coupons, special sales, mailing list subscriptions, list of products and services.

Tour information: Museums, zoos, art galleries and tourist sites.

QR codes are a shortcut. You scan the image with your smartphone's camera (on an iPhone, Android or Blackberry, for example), and you're immediately taken to a webpage. Or you hear music, a story, or see a video. Or have information transferred to your cell phone.

You and QR Codes

POINT ON A CODE   TAKE A PICTURE   DECODING   WEBSITE

Image courtesy of Wikipedia

How do I scan and decode a QR code?

1. Download a reader from your mobile phone's application store. iPhone, Android, Blackberry, Windows and Symbian (Nokia) all offer barcode scanning applications for free.

   There are other reader applications, often with more features, for which you can pay, if you wish. Some of them specialize in comparison shopping so that after decoding a standard UPC 1d barcode, your phone can show you a list of stores (both online and nearby brick and mortar stores) that carry the product and their various prices.

   Once you have downloaded the application, you will have it on your phone permanently, though you may occasionally be notified that there are updates.

2. Start the barcode reader application.

3. Hold the camera phone in front of/over the QR code until you can see it in your viewer. When the camera has the symbol in focus and recognizes that it is a QR code, it will automatically take its picture; you don't even have to press a button. The reader application will

then automatically decode the symbol and take whatever action the code instructs.

What happens when I scan a QR code?

The QR code contains data which either directly provides you with information or carries out an action. For example, a QR code that contains a web address (URL) will show you the web link on your phone's display and ask you if you want to use your browser. If you say yes, it will take you to that address on the web. (Some applications will not even ask but instead take you immediately to the website.)

Readers

How do I find the right QR code reader for my phone?

There are many readers for each phone. One way to find a reader that works for your phone is to use your mobile device to go to:

www.percentmobile.com/getqr

At the website, you'll see a list of appropriate readers for your specific phone, whether it's an Android, iPhone, Blackberry, Nokia or Windows Mobile. Select one of the readers and automatically download it to your phone.

Another site that offers a similar service is:

http://m.qmcodes.com/reader

Google recommends for its Favorite Places decals that Android users download "Barcode Scanner", and that iPhone users should try "QuickMark" (www.quickmark.com.tw). Google also suggests that Neoreader (www.neoreader.com) and BeeTagg (www.beetagg.com) work well with a number of different phones. I-nigma (www.i-nigma.com) is another reader that has great success decoding QR codes.

Android

When we last checked there were 28 free QR code readers at the Android Market (https://market.android.com/), and there are likely far more by the time you're reading this.

Barcode Scanner

We recommend Barcode Scanner for the Android. It was developed and is continually enhanced by Google, which also developed and maintains the Android's operating system. You can download it at the Android Market.

If you prefer another QR code reader, go to the Android Market and search for "QR code".

BeeTagg

www.beetagg.com

BeeTagg's reader scans BeeTagg codes, QR codes and Datamatrix. Use your mobile phone's browser to go to http://get.beetagg.com and follow the directions to install it on your phone.

I-Nigma

www.i-nigma.mobi

Use your mobile phone to go to http://www.i-nigma.mobi/. If i-Nigma has a QR code reader for your particular handset, it will tell you how to easily install it on your phone. The application scans QR codes and Datamatrix, as well as common 1d barcodes.

Blackberry

BeeTagg

www.beetagg.com

BeeTagg's reader scans BeeTagg codes, QR codes and Datamatrix. Use your mobile phone's browser to go to http://get.beetagg.com and follow the directions to install it on your phone.

I-Nigma

www.i-nigma.mobi

If i-Nigma has a QR code reader for your particular handset, it will tell you how to easily install it on your phone. Scans QR codes and Datamatrix, as well as common 1d barcodes.

iPhone

When we last checked, there were at least 40 free QR code readers for the iPhone. With its Favorite Places project, Google recommends QuickMark for the iPhone. It also suggests NeoReader as a good iPhone reader.

BeeTagg

www.beetagg.com

BeeTagg's reader scans BeeTagg codes, QR codes and Datamatrix. Use your mobile phone's browser to go to http://get.beetagg.com and follow the directions to install it on your phone.

I-Nigma

www.i-nigma.mobi

If i-Nigma has a QR code reader for your particular handset, it will tell you how to easily install it on your phone. The application scans QR codes and Datamatrix, as well as common 1d barcodes.

NeoReader

www.neoreader.com

NeoReader is free and works with Datamatrix and Aztec codes as well as QR codes. Once you have it installed on your phone, you can test it out on examples at the NeoReader website.

QuickMark

www.quickmark.com.tw

Reads QR codes as well as Datamatrix and standard 1d barcodes.

Keeps scanned codes in a history for your later use. Includes a QR code generator so you can create your own.

Nokia

BeeTagg

www.beetagg.com

BeeTagg's reader scans BeeTagg codes, QR codes and Datamatrix. Use your mobile phone's browser to go to http://get.beetagg.com and follow the directions to install it on your phone.

I-Nigma

www.i-nigma.mobi

Use your mobile phone to go to http://www.i-nigma.mobi/. If i-Nigma has a QR code reader for your particular handset, it will tell you how to easily install it on your phone. Scans QR codes and Datamatrix, as well as common 1d barcodes.

Windows Mobile

Microsoft Tag

www.microsoft.com/tag

Microsoft's reader scans and decodes only its own proprietary Microsoft Tag. It does not read QR codes. To get the reader for your phone, open the internet browser on your mobile phone and visit http://gettag.mobi. The reader is available for Windows Mobile phones, as well as iPhone, Blackberry and some Symbian phones.

QuickMark

www.quickmark.com.tw

Reads QR codes as well as Datamatrix and standard 1d barcodes.

Keeps scanned codes in a history for your later use. Includes a QR code generator so that you can create your own.

Can I decode QR codes on my desktop computer?

If you're using your desktop or laptop computer and see a QR code that you would like to decode, you don't need a mobile phone to decode it. Google has an *online* decoder at http://zxing.org/w/decode.jspx You can either enter the URL for the image, or upload the image as a file.

Here's how Google's decoder displays the information it finds. It's not elegant, but it works. This is for the QR code shown on my personal website, which is the same as on my business card and includes all my contact information including name, phone, email, website and Twitter address. The full URL for the image, which I entered into Google's online decoder, is:

http://www.westsong.com/mickwinter/files/mickfinalqrsmfortext.jpg

Raw textMECARD:N:Mick Winter;TEL:
+17073075466;EMAIL:mick@mickwinter.com;NOTE:twitter/mickwinter;
URL:www.mickwinter.com;;

Raw bytes20 53 ec 44 d3 33 e9 fd 24 10 69 63 6b 20 57 69 6e 74 65 72 3b
54 45 4c 3a 2b 10 2c aa b6 af 28 48 96 76 8a 9a 82 92 98 74 da d2 c6 d6
80 da d2 c6 d6 ee d2 dc e8 ca e4 5c c6 de da 76 9c 9e a8 8a 74 e8 ee d2
e8 e8 ca e4 5e da d2 c6 d6 ee d2 dc e8 ca e4 76 aa a4 98 74 ee ee ee 5c da
d2 c6 d6 ee d2 dc e8 ca e4 5c c6 de da 76 76 00 ec 11 ec 11 ec 11 ec 11 ec
11 ec 11 ec 11 ec 11 ec 11

Barcode formatQR_CODE

Parsed Result TypeADDRESSBOOK

Parsed ResultMick Winter +17073075466 mick@mickwinter.com
www.mickwinter.com twitter/mickwinter

Making QR Codes

Why make a QR Code?

Because a QR code can link mobile phone users to information or entertainment that they can't otherwise get—at the *time* and at the *location*.

* Give them information they want or need but which isn't readily available.
* Help them save or make money.
* Entertain them.

Can I make color QR codes?

Most people report that black and white works best for QR codes, although some use of color is successful. There are some online code generators that will let you use color. If you wish, experiment and test it well. Make sure that you use solid colors, and that the contrast between the two colors, or between one color and the background, is great.

What resolution should QR codes have?

QR codes are scalable in size and resolution, so you can modify them to your needs. It's generally recommended not to make them smaller than 100 pixels across.

Can someone make a QR code for me?

If you wish, as there are many services that will make QR codes for you for a fee. Since you can make your own at no cost, we suggest that if you hire someone to do it for you, you choose someone who will also include various support services such as design, printing, website assistance, and analytics (tracking use of the QR code to see when and where it's most effective).

A professional service can create QR codes as well as a variety of other types of barcodes, including their own proprietary codes. The analytics data that they provide can include such information as where and when the codes were used, the type of mobile devices used, and the telephone carriers, as well as frequency of use and percentage of a specific code's use within a large multi-code campaign.

How can I make my own QR Codes?

You can use a free online QR Code "generator" at any of the following websites to make your own QR codes.

BeeTagg

http://generator.beetagg.com/

From Swiss company BeeTagg. Creates their own BeeTagg code as well as QR codes and Datamatrix codes for URL, Facebook, RSS feed, Contacts, YouTube, and eBay.

Delivr

http://delivr.com/qr-code-generator

Delivr offers a built-in URL shortener as well as the ability to encode URLs, text, SMS, contact information, email addresses, RSS feeds, and more than 20 social networks, including Digg, Delicious, StumbleUpon, YouTube, Twitter, Facebook, MySpace, eBay and LinkedIn..

Google

Google Zxing

http://zxing.appspot.com/generator/

From Google. Zxing is the barcode reader used by many QR code readers for Android phones. Creates codes for URL, SMS, phone, text, geolocation, email, calendar event, and contact information.

Goo.gl

www.goo.gl

You can also use Google's URL-shortening service to make QR codes. Enter a long URL and see the short URL that results. Click on "Details" and you'll see analytics information for the new URL and a QR code that links to that URL. Be aware that, as Google points out, all URLs and their analytics are viewable by the public. If you want confidentiality, use one of the other analytic services mentioned in this book.

Kaywa

http://qrcode.kaywa.com/

From Japanese company Kaywa. Creates QR codes for URL, phone, SMS and text.

QR Code/Datamatrix Generator

http://keremerkan.net/php-qr-code-and-data-matrix-generator/

This excellent QR code generator does 15 different code actions, and can create symbols in color.

Currently you can do the following with QR codes created at this site:

- You can browse to a website.
- You can bookmark a website.
- You can make a phone call.
- You can send a short message.
- You can send an e-mail.
- You can create a vCard (v2.1 or v3.0) with coordinates to add a contact to your device.
- You can create a meCard to add a contact to your device.
- You can create a vCalendar event to add to your calendar.
- You can open location coordinates in Google Maps on your device.
- You can create `market://` URLs for searching for publishers or packages on Market app for Android.
- You can create special `youtube://` URLs.
- You can fetch and encode the latest tweet of a Twitter user.
- You can create a mobile URL to tweet on Twitter.
- You can create a mobile URL to update your Facebook status.
- You can read plain or free formatted text on your device.

ScanLife

www.scanlife.com

ScanLife offers a barcode reader application (available at www.getscanlife.com) as well as a 2d code generator on their website. You can create QR codes, Datamatrix codes and EZcodes, and ScanLife can provide analytics to track use of your codes. Free for personal use, charge for business use.

How do I enter text into the QR code generator?

With most QR code generators, it's very simple to fill out the form for the code's content. They'll display very clearly on your screen exactly what you need to enter, and any technical language such as "http://" will be built-in.

However, just so you know, and in case you need them sometime, we provide full instructions in Appendix C on page 122 .

Can I create QR codes with my mobile phone?

The answer now is yes. It's no longer necessary to have a desktop computer in order to create QR codes. Most phones have one or more applications that will make the codes; sometimes it's the same application that scans codes. As an alternative, you can also use your mobile phone's browser to go to a website and make a QR code there using the application.. Search your mobile phone's application store for "QR code" or "QR code generator" to see if there's one for your phone.

Rules of Thumb for making QR codes

Testing

When you're testing your barcodes, make sure you use several different phones and that at least one of them is a *low-resolution* camera phone. Chances are, if it works on the less sophisticated, and probably older, camera phone, it will work on newer, higher-resolution phones.

Color

While codes can be created with some colors, it's important that the contrast between them is very high. Safest is to simply use black and white. Otherwise, test very carefully with a number of different phones and readers (as you should be doing anyhow.)

Logos

Standard QR codes will seldom work with a small logo in the middle. If a logo is essential, use one of the proprietary systems such as BeeTagg (see above).

Number of Characters

Although QR codes will handle several thousand characters, codes with many characters are suitable mainly for sophisticated QR code readers, such as used by manufacturing and inventory control. If you are creating codes for use by mobile phones, keep the number of characters as small as possible, generally 20-40. And test.

Size

While it's preferable sometimes to have a very unobtrusive QR code—on a business card for example—they should seldom be smaller than 2.5 cm (1 inch). Any smaller and they will be very difficult for many camera phones to read. Yes, newer phones with better cameras can read QR codes as small as 0.5 inches, but you probably don't want to restrict access to only those users with the newest phones.

Firefox Extension

If you use Firefox as your web browser, you can add on an extension called *Mobile Barcoder* which will let you automatically create a QR code for the URL of the current page in your browser. You can save the QR code on your mobile phone, post it on a blog or website, or send it to friends.

Mobile Barcoder

> https://addons.mozilla.org/en-US/firefox/addon/2780

WordPress Extension

If you operate a blog created with WordPress, you can use a plugin to create QR codes for your blog posts. To see all currently available plugins, go to:

> www.wordpress.org/extend/plugins/

and search for "QR code".

How do I convince someone to scan the QR code I made?

An excellent question. Here are some tips.

- **Mobile users are impulsive!**

  Give them a reason to act on the spur of the moment. Make it interesting. Make it intriguing. Make it fun. It may be appropriate to tell them exactly what they will get, such as nutritional information for a menu item. But whenever possible, give hints that are specific enough to make them willing to take the time (although it's very brief) to scan the code. Make it look like it's worth their time. If they don't scan the symbol, all the effort you spent on the information that's waiting for them at other end goes for nothing.

- **Remember your goal**

  Just as the QR code is a portal between the physical world and the virtual world, it's also a link between the user's goal and your goal. Their goal must be in synch with yours. They want something; you want them to get that something. Both of you benefit from the exchange.

- **Give them a good reason**

  Make sure it's worth the mobile phone user's time to scan the QR code. Don't duplicate what they're already seeing.

  For example, I once proposed that a restaurant put a QR code in their front window to link to their menu. Not a bad idea if it weren't for the fact that they already had a printed menu in the window. Linking to the current menu would have been redundant; linking to what *can't* be seen wouldn't be. For example, the QR code could link to a special two-for-one coupon. Or it could link to (presumably positive) online reviews of the restaurant. This would give people trying to decide whether to walk into the restaurant some information that is not otherwise available.

  However...linking to a menu isn't a totally bad idea. A restaurant can encourage its patrons to bookmark a link to their current but ever-changing menu in their phone's browser. That way regular patrons can always see what's available when they're in the area.

- **Make it easy for them**

  Use a short address for the website. Either create a short URL yourself, or use a URL shortener such as www.tinyurl.com, www.goo.gl or www.bit.ly. The shorter the URL, the smaller and/or easier to read is the QR code symbol. Easier to read means faster and less error-prone scanning.

- **Make it readable when they get there**

  If your QR code is linked to a webpage, make sure that webpage is mobile-friendly. Your website can:

  - be created strictly as a mobile website
  - detect that it is being accessed by a mobile device and re-direct that device to a specific mobile *section* of the website
  - allow the phone user to choose to transfer to the mobile area of the website through a link on the home page

Remember:

- **Worthwhile** - It should be useful, offering the user something of value. It can provide information that is relevant to the mobility (location-specific, convenient, fast, timely), or that has actual value (money saving, money making, free). And any information that you provide should be absolutely up-to-date. Timeliness is one of the most important reasons for the use of QR codes.

- **Simple and fun** - It should be simple to execute or understand, yet actively engage the user.

- **Unique to mobile** - It should be unique, something that can not be received in any other convenient way. Unique to the moment, unique to the location. Make them feel that they're part of a special group because they're using their phone to gain something unique.

Where can I put QR Codes?

You'll find detailed information in our A to Z section, but in the meantime here's a brief list:

- On websites
- Into PowerPoint and other presentation software
- On stickers to place on objects, buildings, signs
- On flyers, newsletters, newspapers

- Onto objects during the manufacturing process
- On T-shirt transfer sheets
- On tattoo transfer paper
- On transparencies for use with projectors
- On books. On covers, inside the book for a link to live information on something the book mentions, or to read about other books on the subject or from the same author or publisher
- In magazines. In ads; next to articles; on cover
- In museums, galleries and zoos. Accompanying art work and exhibits
- In newspapers. In ads, next to articles, in classified ads
- On billboards
- On posters
- On bus cards
- In television commercials
- In television program (for more information about program, star, etc.)
- On products: Parts, appliances, food packaging, DVDs, CDs, books, magazines, beverage containers
- On food products and food packaging
- On jewelry
- On coffee mugs and glasses
- On vehicles

In short, the only limit is your own imagination.

QR Code Analytics

A number of services provide QR code analytics, meaning they can track information about how your QR codes are used, who uses them, what type of mobile device is used, and so on.

Google

Google Analytics

www.google.com/analytics

Google Analytics isn't specifically designed to track QR codes but because it can analyze activity on any webpage, if you have webpages that are reached only via QR codes, it will be clear how effective your QR codes have been.

Goo.gl

www.goo.gl

Use Google's URL shortener and you'll get a shorter URL, a QR code that points to that URL, and analytics on the use of the URL. Be aware that the URL and analytics are publicly viewable.

Google Places

www.google.com/places

Create a Google Places account for your business and as a plus Google will automatically provide you with a QR code and QR code poster, as well as analytics on traffic to your website.

SPARQCode

www.sparqcode.com

SPARQCode provides a free QR code generator as well as free tracking for up to 1,000 scans per campaign. Premium accounts provide a variety of other marketing services and more detailed analytics for larger amounts of data.

MyQR

www.myqr.co

MyQR provides free tracking data as well as a free QR code generator that lets you create codes in black and white or with different foreground and background colors.

Percent Mobile

www.percentmobile.com

PercentMobile tracks extensive analytics of mobile traffic to your website. Offers both free and Professional plans.

QRMe

www.qrme.co.uk/

QRMe lets you create QR codes at no cost. These codes pass through QRMe's servers so that, if you wish, you can change their targets so that they point to different pages. Their service provides the usual analytical data on use and users.

ScanLife

www.scanlife.com

Lets you create codes and then obtain analytical data on how, where and when the codes are scanned. Both free and premium accounts are offered.

Google and QR Codes

Google Places

Google is one of the greatest promoters of QR codes. Their Google Places campaign is exposing people to QR codes at hundreds of thousands of locations around the United States. But Google has other applications as well.

Google's use of QR codes for its "Favorite Places" program jumpstarted the use of QR codes in the United States. They sent out QR code decals to 100,000 businesses around the country that were the most popular on Google's Local Business Center program. Businesses selected as Favorite Places display these in their store or restaurant windows. Prospective customers can scan the codes and read about the business and its customer reviews before deciding whether or not to enter the premises.

For Business Owners

Here's how Google announced their QR code program on their blog:

Want to become a Favorite Place on Google?

If you've seen a decal that says "We're a Favorite Place on Google" on a window near you, you may wonder how they got it and what you can do to get a decal for your business. Here's how it works:

- **Businesses unlock their free business listing** with Google's Local Business Center, allowing them to enhance the content of their listings with photos, correct hours, coupons and more. This also tells Google that the business' location is correct, so we can send a window decal if the business is popular enough.

- **People search for local businesses** on Google.com and Google Maps, more than anywhere else.

- **Google identifies the most popular local businesses** based on how many Google users looked for more information about a business, looked for driving directions to the business, and more. Business owners can get this data about their business after they claim their free listing at www.google.com/lbc.

We [Google] plan to periodically send out new waves of window decals to businesses that meet our criteria. You can make your business eligible by claiming your listing with Google at https://www.google.com/accounts/NewAccount - *Google*

Here's a short video that shows the Google Favorite Place's window decals in action.

http://bit.ly/googlefaves

For Customers

What if you could decide where to shop, eat or hang out, with a little help from local Google users?

It might take you a while to ask them all, so to make it easier we've launched a new effort to send window decals to over 100,000 local businesses in the U.S. that have been the most sought out and researched on Google.com and Google Maps. We're calling these businesses the

"Favorite Places on Google" and you'll now start to find them in over 9,000 towns and cities, in all 50 states. You can also explore a sample of the Favorite Places in 20 of the largest U.S. cities at google.com/favoriteplaces. Each window decal has a unique bar code, known as a QR code that you can scan with any of hundreds of mobile devices — including iPhone, Android-powered phones, BlackBerry and more — to take you directly to that business's Place Page on your mobile phone. With your mobile phone and these new decals, you can easily go up to a storefront and immediately find reviews, get a coupon if the business is offering one or star a business as a place you want to remember for the future. Soon, you'll be able to leave a review on the mobile page as well, just like on your desktop.

To scan the codes, you'll need a phone with a camera and an app that can read QR codes. For Android-powered devices, including the Droid by Motorola, we recommend using the free Barcode Scanner app. For iPhone, we have found the $1.99 QuickMark app to work best, and starting today, we're partnering with QuickMark to offer the app for free for the first 40,000 downloads. For other devices, we recommend searching for "QR reader" in your app marketplace, if it has one, or searching for the model of your phone and [qr reader] on Google. BeeTagg and NeoReader are two other apps that we've found to work well with the decals.

This launch is part of our overall effort — online and offline — to provide you with the best local business results whenever you're trying to figure out where to go, whether it's a trendy Cuban restaurant in Philly, a comics shop in L.A., a hip hotel in NYC or a little bit of photographic history in Rochester, N.Y.

We plan to periodically send out new waves of window decals to qualifying businesses. If you own or manage a business and were selected as a Favorite Place, you may have already received your decal or, for most of you, it will arrive by mail in the next one to two weeks. If you weren't selected in this round, your first step is to claim your listing with Google's Local Business Center for free. That will help us determine that your business information is correct. Then, you can enhance your local business listing by adding enhanced content like photos and videos.

To explore a gallery of several hundred Favorite Places in 20 U.S. cities, to learn more about how to use the QR codes and to find out how your business can get involved, check out google.com/favoriteplaces.

Update *on 12/18*: If your phone does not support the mobile version of Place Pages, you will be taken to the mobile version of the Google homepage upon scanning the QR code. The QR code itself is correct and should take you to the mobile Place Page on supported devices. - *Google*

"Google Places" Poster with QR Code

Any business can now become a "Google Place" (not necessarily a "Favorite Place" but hopefully that will come for you over time). If you haven't yet registered your business with Google, go to http://www.google.com/places.

"Google Places" is the name of Google's former "Local Business Center". At Places you're able to manage all your online business information which includes your location, map, directions, phone number, hours, regular website, email, photos, and even reviews. Plus you can post coupons and live updates, and see how you're doing with a performance "dashboard" that shows such information as number of visitors, when they visited, and the search terms they used to find you. Your dashboard even displays your own business QR Code that directs mobile users directly to your Google Places website. You can copy it for your own use on printed material. You can even print out a color "We're on the Map" poster that already contains your QR code. And it's all free.

Google Goggles

Google Goggles actually dispenses with the need for QR codes or any type of barcode and simply analyzes a picture of something. You use your camera phone to take the picture, Goggles analyzes the image, compares it to its huge and ever-growing database of images, and comes back with information that it considers directly relevant to the image you have just photographed. As of this writing, Google Goggles works with: landmarks, books, contact information, artwork, places, wine labels and logos.

When Google released Goggles in its Beta (test) version, it did not provide the capability to analyze photographs of people. But Google does have that technology. It acquired it when it some years ago acquired a company called *Neven*. When it works out concerns of personal privacy, it will undoubtedly begin to analyze images of people as well as buildings and objects. In fact, it may have done so by the time you read this.

The advantage of Google Goggles is that it can provide information about almost anything, assuming that that *anything*—or something very similar to that anything—is in Google's database. What it cannot do is provide the specific information that you want delivered and *only* that information you want delivered. That is the current advantage of QR codes.

More information is at the website:
www.google.com/mobile/goggles

Mobile Web

Mobile Web refers to those websites or areas of a web that are accessible—and *friendly*—to mobile devices, whether phones, notebooks or tablets (such as Apple's iPad) using web browsers. According to the International Telecommunications Union, in 2008 for the first time the total number of mobile web users exceeded the total number of desktop computer-based web users. While many people use only a mobile device to access the web, this fact obviously includes those who access the web through both mobile and desktop. But the importance of the mobile web is very clear, including the fact that many billions of dollars of merchandise (music, ringtones, games, and online shopping) are sold through mobile phones every year. This awareness has even reached the White House in Washington, D.C., which now has a mobile website at http://m.whitehouse.gov/.

Should I use the .mobi Extension?

The .mobi (for "mobile") top-level domain was proposed specifically for the mobile Internet by a consortium of companies including Google, Microsoft, Nokia, Samsung, and Vodafone. The goal was to ensure a consistent interface and experience on mobile websites. So far, it doesn't appear to have worked as the use of the .mobi extension is not frequent, although this could change. In practice, companies and others are simply using their existing *.com* domain names, and making their websites smart enough to detect mobile devices and deliver them a mobile-friendly website.

If you want a .mobi website, fine. Get one. But it probably makes sense only for a website designed to appeal specifically—and only—to users of mobile devices. The best solution is to create a .com (.org, .net, .info) website which serves both desktop and mobile users.

Mobile Websites

While the purpose of this book isn't to help you design websites, we will discuss mobile websites since that's what your QR codes will, and should, likely link to.

If you convince someone to scan your QR code in order to bring them to your website, you'd better have a friendly greeting waiting for them. That means a mobile-friendly website; one that displays well on their phone or other mobile device and provides easy navigation, getting them exactly where they want to go as quickly as possible. Since that currently means with mobile phones (but not necessarily with tablets and notebooks) that your small-display webpage "real estate" is minimal, you should focus on providing only what is absolutely essential to a mobile user.

On a desktop computer there's generally time for a user to wander around, look at pretty graphics, and discover new interesting things. However, the mobile user wants information Right Now—fast and relevant. "Relevant" usually means both timely and location-specific. "I'm standing at such-and-such intersection. I want to know where and when the next showing of such-and-such movie is." Or "Where can I find the best deal on the new Sandra Bullock DVD? I need it for a birthday party in 30 minutes."

They might also want your website to "Amuse me for seven minutes until my bus arrives" or "Where nearby can I get a quick lunch?" or "Quick. I need a map to your store" or "I've got five minutes to call your store before my girlfriend shows up. What's your phone number?"

Mobile Website Design Tips

- Visitors will go to your mobile website for specific information or entertainment. Make sure they can find what they want quickly and easily.

- Skip the graphics, animations and all the fun things your programmer wanted to put in your desktop website, and just focus on the essential information. Of course if your website's purpose is graphics or video, that's different. But present it in a way that's easy and enjoyable to find and view on a small screen. Keep your images small.

- Keep the number of page levels to a minimum. It's confusing enough on a desktop PC to go up and down through a number of levels of pages. It's even worse on a mobile phone. If you have so much content that it's absolutely necessary to have a number of levels, at least have the most important—and the most requested—information on the top one or two levels.

- Make selecting an option very easy. Entering text on a mobile phone is seldom easy and is very error-prone. Minimize the need to type text into fields and maximize the ability to simply press an option. Keep enough space between links so that it is easy to press only the correct link.

- Make it very clear where the cursor is; it's often hard to tell on a mobile phone. Make the text highlighted by the cursor stand out. Use text and/or background color to create a very strong contrast between the regular text and the highlighted text.

- Don't put a lot of navigation links and menus on your mobile website. Keep it slim. On other than your home page, unless you have a very good reason for exceptions, keep your links to basics such as "Back", "Next" and "Home".

- Test. Test on your own mobile phone. Test on the phones of everyone at your business. Test on your family's and friends' phones. Use an online mobile website testing service such as MobiReady (www.ready.mobi). Then pay attention to the results of the tests and re-design your website until it keeps almost everyone happy and works on a large variety of mobile platforms, most importantly iPhone, Android, Nokia/Symbian, Windows Mobile.

- Include the mobile address (and a QR code) in your email signature.

- Place a link (and also a QR code) on your desktop website for visitors to go to your mobile website. Repeat the QR code on your mobile site so that if someone arrives there by linking from a desktop screen, they can scan the QR code and bookmark your URL.

Example: Look at Wikipedia's mobile-friendly website. It's the little brother of Wikipedia's regular desktop website, stripped down with no images and a simple search box. All articles are split into multiple pages.

http://mobile.wikipedia.org

How do I *mobilize* an existing desktop website?

"Mobilize" here means simply to make your existing desktop website "mobile-friendly." It certainly sounds easier to "mobilize" your existing large-screen desktop website than to create a new small-screen mobile website from the ground up. After all, you've already spent a lot of time, and perhaps a lot of money, creating your existing website. Doesn't it make more sense to just tweak it a little?

Well, yes and no. It depends on the website. If you want to try turning your mobile-indifferent, or even mobile-snarly, website into a nice warm and fuzzy mobile-friendly website, here are some suggestions.

Google Mobile Website Converter

www.google.com/gwt/n

Even though it's a Google creation, it's still so unofficial it doesn't have a name. But it can do a quick and dirty conversion of your desktop website into a mobile website. Try it and see if what it produces is satisfactory.

Simply enter the URL for your website, select whether to Hide Images or keep them in, and click on Go. You'll now see a mobile version of your website.

If the results are unsatisfactory, as they have been for most of my own websites, go on to the next option below. But if it works for your site, and what you see displayed is satisfactory, save the URL displayed at the top of your browser.

The URL you see displayed will be very, very long. Copy it, go to a URL shortener such as www.tinyurl.com or www.bit.ly and use that service to shorten your URL down to something manageable. You can then use the new shortened URL when you create the QR code that will direct people to your mobile website.

Instant Mobilizer

www.instantmobilizer.com/

If you want to have instant, on-the-fly mobilization of your website, and you're willing to do it with a .mobi domain, you could try this paid service. It operates only through hosting/name selling services such as GoDaddy.

Mippin Mobilizer

www.mippin.com/web/maker/mobilize.jsp

Mippin will take your RSS feed and turn it into a mobile website at no charge. Enter your URL, select either List or Gallery view, upload your logo, customize your color scheme, preview the website and you're done. Mippin also has a plugin for WordPress.

Mofuse

www.mofuse.com

Create a mobile website from your RSS feed or start a new one from scratch. Mofuse has a number of levels, starting at a low monthly cost and increasing based on the size, number of visitors, and features of your site(s). Used by a number of high-profile organizations.

How do I create a Mobile Website?

If mobilizing your desktop website didn't work out, the following sites let you create, from the ground up, a website focused totally on mobile phones.

MobiSiteGalore

www.mobisitegalore.com

mobiSiteGalore is a mobile website builder that allows you to use logos, customized titles, multiple page names, images, and a variety of other features. There's a low monthly cost for basic page and services. If you wish to remove their company name from the top and bottom of your webpage, add more or unlimited pages, include Google AdSense ads, or add other features, the price increases accordingly.

MobiTen

www.mobiten.com

Let's you quickly ("10 minutes or less") create a mobile website designed to work with most smartphones, including iPhone, Android and Blackberry. A basic website is free, and there is a charge for the Pro version which offers additional storage space and other features.

Mofuse

www.mofuse.com

Start a new mobile website from scratch (or create one from your RSS feed). Mofuse has a number of levels, starting at a low monthly cost and increasing based on the size, number of visitors, and features of your site(s). Used by a number of high-profile organizations.

Winksite

www.winksite.com

Winksite has a strong focus on community, with forums, chats, surveys and a blog. The service lets you include mobile ads in your website and keep 100% of any revenue. Connect with blogs and Twitter. Free.

Wirenode

www.wirenode.com

Create new mobile websites at no charge for up to three sites. Can include RSS feed, Google Maps, message board, gallery, Twitter and other features. For a custom domain name or to remove Wirenode's ads, there is a monthly charge.

Zinadoo

www.zinadoo.com

Zinadoo provides free hosting, site creation and use of the zinadoo.mobi domain. If you wish to have your own .mobi domain name, or to remove ads from your website, there are additional charges.

Mobile Website Testing

You'll want to test your mobile website thoroughly before you turn it loose on the world. Here's a free, but thorough, testing website that rates your website according to best practice and industry standards.

MobiReady

www.ready.mobi

Just enter the URL of the page you want to check, and click on Go. You'll quickly see the Overall Rating, as well as more detailed information, and further tests you can conduct.

How You Can Use QR Codes

Actions and Information Checklist

A QR Code is your—and your customers'—portal to a wide variety of actions and information. The code gives your mobile phone instructions to carry out various tasks or to display or access specific information. Here is a list of key actions and information that QR codes can provide.

About

Downloads text, audio or video about an object, your location, or your surroundings, particularly useful in tourist areas, galleries and museums, and for real estate information.

Audio

Downloads and plays an audio recording such as a song or song clip, podcast, audiobook, ringtone, or streaming audio from local or web radio station.

Calendar Event

Places an event into your phone's calendar

Contact

Places contact information such as business card information into your phone's contact list.

Document

Downloads a document such as an article, letter, magazine, newspaper, paper, spreadsheet, slide presentation, menu, manual, or e-book; a discount or instant winner coupon, or a contest entry form.

Dynamic Tweets

Displays real-time tweets from Twitter, by searching for key words and #hashtags.

eBay

Links to items for sale on eBay

Email

Places an email address into your phone's email *To:* field.

Facebook

Links to personal, group, event and business webpages.

Image

Downloads a photograph or other image for viewing or for use as wallpaper on your phone's display.

Link

Shows a web link (URL) and asks if you want to use your browser to see the website. On some phones it may automatically go to a website without asking first. You can also bookmark the URL on your phone's browser.

Map

Displays a map showing the location of a business or point of interest, or the location where you're standing when you scan the code. Can display nearby restaurants, restrooms, shops and places of interest and give you necessary navigation directions, either with text or audio.

Menu

Lets you select an option from the menu items.

Payment

Lets you or others buy an item through PayPal, Amazon Payments, Google Checkout, or other transaction system.

Phone

Initiates a phone call by automatically placing a phone number into your phone's dialer.

Search

Automatically uses a search engine to search for the subject already placed in the Subject field.

Shopping

Downloads information on a product's prices, reviews, and where it is available for purchase.

SMS

Automatically places a number into your SMS (text messaging) address field, and may also include a ready-to-go message for you to send. Can also be used to automatically subscribe to text alerts, email lists, or other types of sign-up.

Social Networking

Connects to, displays posts from, or lets you make posts to any of the popular social networking sites.

Text

Displays plain text which can be, for example, a message, pet information, GPS geocaching, or clues for a treasure or scavenger hunt.

Tickets

Displays a boarding pass, movie or performance admission ticket, discount or free coupon, or event registration pass.

Timely

Downloads movie and TV schedules; flight, train, bus or ferry schedules, status and routes; stock prices; weather forecasts; surf or ski conditions; headline and updated news; sports scores; shopping specials; event calendars, horoscopes, or traffic conditions.

Twitter

Links to Twitter account page or to Twitter #hashtags.

Video

Downloads and plays a video recording such as a YouTube video or movie trailer, or a video related to your present location.

Webcam

Links to a webcam that displays real-time visual information about a location.

Important Things to Remember

- ### Mobile-friendly websites

  We cannot overemphasize that if you are linking to websites, those websites *must* be mobile-friendly. That means they must be formatted in a manner so that they are easy to see, read and use on all mobile phones. In fact, any information linked to through QR codes must be easily readable and usable by mobile phones. If it isn't, there is little value in using the QR code.

- ### Only when needed or enhances information

  In most cases, if the information can be delivered as well or better in another manner, there's unlikely to be an advantage to using QR codes. Where QR codes are most useful is for bookmarking websites on a mobile phone, for information that is location-specific, for real-time information which changes frequently, and for uses when the phone's owner is moving from one location to another.

- ### Avoid dense QR codes

  Keep the URL as short as possible. In most cases, use a URL shortener such as www.bit.ly. The less data in the QR code, the easier it is for a barcode reader to decode it accurately.

The A to Z of QR Codes

Note: While you're of course welcome to read this section straight through, it's designed primarily for you to be able to easily find your own specific interests, business and other uses.

Academic Papers and Journals

Journal articles in print can include QR codes that link to essential or related information such as other articles by the author or to source or supplemental material. This can be particularly useful when the article was produced in conjunction with a physical or digital artifact, as in practice-based research, which can be displayed as images, audio or video. (See also Appendix E – Academia on page 129.)

Advertising/Public Relations

Printed Material

Place QR codes in newspapers, magazines, brochures, flyers and any other hardcopy advertising or press releases. Codes can link to editorial content, videos, testimonials and reviews, phone applications, wallpaper images, or purchase options.

Television

Display QR code throughout an entire commercial to give viewers time to pick up their phones and scan. Viewers can scan the code equally as well on a television screen as on printed media. QR codes can even be an integral part of the commercial's storyline itself, so that the narration, dialogue or camera emphasizes the code, thereby directing the viewer's attention even more to the code. This direction will be less necessary as QR codes become commonly accepted by the viewing public.

Outdoor

For safety reasons, QR codes should be used only on outdoor advertising that is aimed at pedestrians, not drivers. Since billboards, lighting and other outdoor displays are obviously location-specific, wherever possible take advantage of the location and its amenities to highlight the advantages of your product.

Radio

There are no audio QR codes yet, but who knows? There's no reason that certain external sounds (music, frequencies or combinations of frequencies), in combination with a mobile phone's microphone and special software, couldn't trigger certain actions by a mobile phone.

New Media

The phrase "new media" basically describes the Internet and the World Wide Web, and their access by desktop computers, laptops, netbooks, tablets, and mobile phones.

Using a QR code on a webpage is generally redundant if the purpose is simply to go to another webpage. That is, having a QR code that contains a URL or other instruction involves a unnecessary coding of that URL or instruction. It is far easier to simply use a hyperlink since, in this case, a plain hyperlink can more simply do anything that a QR code can do.

However, where a QR code on a desktop screen *does* make sense is when you want to initiate an action that involves a mobile phone. Examples include scanning a QR code to enter contact information on your phone, automatically trigger a phone call or email address, or bookmark a webpage for future access. It is also the easiest way to download something *to* your phone, including music, wallpaper, ringtones, documents, photographs, map locations, e-tickets, videos, coupons and almost all of the other actions and information listed above in "Actions and Information".

In short, if you as an advertiser want to move something from the Internet to mobile phones, the QR code is the easiest way for your user to do it. Using a QR code is also the easiest way for users to vote or otherwise indicate their preference for something such as a song, a product, a political candidate, or any other option.

For example, Adidas conducted an in-store campaign that enabled customers to vote for their favorite color in an Adidas shoe. They could scan the code for a particular color and then be taken to a website where viewing would count as a vote for that color.

Airlines

Paperless ticketing and boarding passes; videos on aircraft safety information, aircraft interior and seating, and check-in procedures. QR codes in in-flight magazines and catalogues can show videos on destinations, as well as on catalogue items which can be purchased using the phone.

Most airlines now give customers the option to receive an electronic boarding pass via email. This digital boarding pass is a QR code. On check-in the customer simply displays the QR code on his phone and the code is then scanned by airline personnel.

QR codes at airport gates can link to the latest information on the airline's flights. Because many passengers in the gate area are seeking entertainment while they wait, airlines can use QR codes to link to videos and short TV programs, as well as to videos on destinations served by the airlines.

Here's a link to a United Airlines menu:

And this links to the real-time status of flights of many different airlines:

Alerts

QR codes can link through a website, email or SMS to subscribe to alerts, such as severe weather warnings, traffic conditions and roadwork, missing persons, or a wide variety of other timely subjects.

Amazon Sales

If you're an Amazon affiliate, you'll want to be able to create QR codes that directly link to the products you sell on Amazon's website. Here's how you do it.

1. You can simply go to the product's webpage and copy the URL at the top of your browser, then use one of the QR code generators we mention in this book to encode it. However, the URL will be long and complicated. Like this:

    http://www.amazon.com/Napa-Valley-Book-EVERYTHING-Californias/dp/096590007X/ref=sr_1_1?ie=UTF8&s=books&qid=1272214756&sr=1-1

    It will also produce a very dense, and for many cameras hard to read, symbol. So to do a shorter version, try the next step.

2. Copy the long Amazon URL and go to a URL shortener website such as www.bit.ly or www.tinyurl.com. Use the service to shorten the URL.

3. Go to any of the QR generators we mention in this book, place the link you just created into the URL field, follow the generator's instructions, and you'll see a QR code containing the shortened link to the Amazon product. If you save the QR code as an image file, you can place it wherever you wish for sales purposes.

Amazon / Barnes & Noble Reviews

Use QR codes for books and other items at garage sales, second-hand stores, or on flyers. This is not recommended for bookstores. Although the reviews are useful, you will be leading prospective customers to an online site where they can likely buy your book at lower cost. Use your own discretion.

Here's a link to reviews on Amazon for a book on the Napa Valley that I wrote several years ago:

Animal Shelters / Humane Societies

Place signs with QR codes in local pet shops and other relevant locations. QR codes link to webpages with information and photos of lost pets, found pets, and pets available for adoption. Shops can sell pet tags with QR codes on them that contain, or link to, information about the pet and its owner.

For example, the QR code below leads to photos and information on cats that are available for adoption at the Napa County Animal Shelter

Appliances

QR codes affixed to home appliances and other products by the manufacturer (or by the owner if not previously affixed by the manufacturer) can link to user manuals, troubleshooting information, and how-to videos.

Here's the manual for the Samsung Vibrant smartphone:

Applications

If you've produced a mobile phone application for your business, organization, band, team, media outlet or other activity, place QR codes on your website and in literature, postcards or any other appropriate place. Phone owners can then scan the codes to download your application directly to their phones.

Art Galleries

Place a QR code with each piece in the gallery right along with the artist's name and other information already displayed. The QR code can provide additional text information, an audio commentary by the artist, or even a slideshow or video showing other works by the same artist, or the artist at work. The code can link to any other information that the artist considers relevant to his or her work. Codes can also link to forums where the gallery or museum visitor can participate in discussions on the artists and their work.

Because mobile phones are now ubiquitous and QR code reader applications for the phones are free, the codes can replace the current costly and inconvenient method of providing gallery and museum visitors with infrared receivers and headsets. No more need to sanitize headsets; no need for gallery or museum staff to deal with the equipment.

QR codes can also be included in catalogues to provide information on the pieces themselves, prices, other work by the artist, and even to purchase items or reproductions.

One art gallery in Minneapolis had a show with nothing but framed QR codes. Each linked to a different, and frequently changing, work of art: images, videos, music and other creations.

Arts and Crafts

Integrate QR codes into various arts and crafts so that customers can learn more about the artist, or see a catalogue of additional items.

Auctions

Post QR code signs in flyers or other printed materials that link to your item or online store and auction sites. Codes can also link to auction site searches, for example to link to all copies of a particular game title.

QR codes in auction catalogues can provide detailed information, photographs or videos of lot items. They can even be used to make bids on the items.

Audio Recordings

A QR code can link directly to a single audio recording (MP3) or to a menu of recordings. Prepare audio recordings to provide information about an object, a location, a home for sale, a message from an artist, musician, clothing designer or the owner of a business, comments from a chef or winemaker, suggestions on the use of a product, or any other information which will enhance the understanding of, or interest in, the subject.

Automobiles

Manufacturers can use QR codes in promotional material, whether in print or on television. The codes can lead to more information, games, music, or contests that promote the automobile.

Automobile dealerships can have QR codes on each automobile, linking to information which will help inform the customer and increase sales, such as videos and TV commercials.

Individuals selling their own used cars through a "street sale" can use a prominent QR code on their vehicle to provide detailed information on the car, as well as its asking price and, if useful, Bluebook price range. QR codes can also be used in classified ads or flyers so that readers can see how the car actually looks.

Kelley Blue Book offers a free Seller's Toolkit that lets you input information online and then generates, among other social network tools, a QR code. Display the QR code on your car, and prospective buyers can scan the code to see complete information on the vehicle including the car's features and current value. (http://www.kbb.com/sellers-toolkit)

Babysitters

When you go out and leave your child with a babysitter, leave not only your phone number but a QR code of that number for your baby sitter, and make sure that the babysitter scans it into his or her phone before you leave the house. Have QR codes for other essential phone numbers as well.

Bands

Place QR codes on the jewel case so that people can easily order their own CD when they see a friend's copy. Place QR codes on flyers and posters that link to your website, performances, song clips, CD purchase, downloads, ringtones, fan sites, YouTube videos, and blog.

Print QR codes on download cards. All a fan has to do is scan the card and instantly download a track.

British singer Labrinth's recording label created a campaign that made extensive use of QR codes. They link to his Facebook page and to his YouTube video which promotes QR codes:

Facebook   **YouTube**

Bars

QR codes on coasters or napkins can link to promotions for the bar itself or for brands of beverages that the bar serves. Link also to events calendar, contests, or "lucky scan gets free drink".

Beverages

Use a QR code on the bottle label to link to online marketing such as video. For products such as specialty beers, link to information about the beer, including the ingredients and brewer's style.

Bird Sounds

On the staff of a park or wildlife preserve with lots of birds? Post QR codes that link to recordings of specific bird calls and songs. Visitors can learn or confirm what they're hearing.

Blogs

Place QR code on flyers or business cards that link to your blog. If your site is such that people will want to read it on their phones, place a QR code on your main page that they can scan to bookmark your URL. Use it for people to subscribe to your RSS feed as well.

Books

Authors: Place QR codes in your book to link to the book's website, to let the reader purchase other books by you, to an audio recording by you, to help readers join your mailing list or discussion forum, to be notified of book signing tours, or to forward a recommendation to a friend that they buy your book. Recommendations can also be posted automatically through Twitter or Facebook.

If relevant, QR codes can be interspersed in the book's content. In non-fiction, or even fiction, codes can link to text, images, audio and video that provide additional background information, historical setting, maps or even clues appropriate to the characters, locations and events in the book. If the QR codes link to websites not under your own control—which is quite likely —you'll want to pick sites that you can presume will have a long life. One such example would be Wikipedia.org

Publishers: Place a QR code on the back cover so people can link to purchase when they see someone else's copy and want their own. Place QR codes in the back content of the book so readers can link to similar books or even your entire catalog. Set up mobile payment so that customers can order and pay for books with their mobile phone. Place a QR code in the book (or at each of the chapters) so that readers can buy an audio version of the book at a reduced charge or even download the audio as a free bonus.

Here's a unique method used in Brazil to create and market a book.

Love/Hate Book

Stickers containing QR codes were spread around the city, inviting people to decode them with their mobile phones. Each sticker revealed a love or hate sentence written by real people on Twitter. Weeks later, these sentences were turned into the world's first Living Book available only at Editoras Online. A book just like the Internet—open source and collaborative. Written in QR codes, it updates itself every seven days with new love and hate sentences written by real people.

The goal was to promote the Brazilian company, located in Rio de Janeiro but which sells only online, and to make it relevant to younger users. There is one QR code on each of the 200 pages, each of which connects to an Internet link which itself randomly chooses a new sentence from Twitter posts. There are 100 pages on Love, 100 pages on Hate.

www.thelivingbook.org

Bookstores

While it might seem natural to use QR codes extensively in your bookstore, use caution. Using a QR code to link to more information about the book and its reviews, such as you get from Amazon or Barnes and Noble, is not likely to be a good idea, since online booksellers can in most cases dramatically undersell a local bookstore. It is possible, however, to link to book reviews and author information in newspapers and magazines, and to online sites that do not themselves sell books. Bookstores can also use QR codes to link to their calendar of author talks and other in-store events.

Bottles

QR codes can be useful on all types of beverage bottles, including wine, beer, liquor and soft drinks. Information provided can include the process of making the beverage and its ingredients (when this information is positive and will enhance sales), as well as contests and discount coupons.

Brochures

Include QR codes to link to websites, audio or even videos, particularly to demonstrate uses, ease of use, testimonials and other supporting material. Travel brochures can show destination videos or, in the case of cruises, display life aboard ship.

Buildings

At a building's entrance, a QR code can provide information on the history of the building, its architect and other facts. It can also link to an internal map of the building and/or a directory of the businesses and offices inside the building.

Buses

Use QR codes inside buses and at bus stops to display schedules, routes, and current status or wait time.

Business Cards

There are two ways to communicate business card information. One is to have it on a website, or at a business-focused web service such as LinkedIn. A QR code on your business card can link to the website and the person who scans the code can see all of your contact information.

The more convenient, but not yet standard, way of communicating contact information is through the use of QR codes and your phone's contact list. Most QR code/barcode readers can decode contact information and even offer (for your approval) to place that information into the appropriate fields in your phone's address book. Google is one company which now gives its employees the option of placing a QR code on their business card.

Here's the code on my own business card:

Calendars

Date-specific QR codes on calendars can link to relevant information, including information on holidays or "This date in history". They can also automatically place this information into the calendars of most mobile phones.

Campgrounds

Signs, flyers and brochures can contain QR codes which link to trail maps, camping regulations, safety warnings, campground registration, flora and fauna information, and activity schedules. The information can be presented as text, audio or video.

Catalogues

QR codes next to each catalogue item can link to detailed information on the product. Photos, audio, videos, coupons and, of course, a "Buy" button.

Cereal Packages

On cereal and other food items, place QR codes that lead to prizes and other rewards, coupons, product-related entertainment, and other external information relevant to the product.

Chain Stores

QR codes in e-newsletters can download discount coupons, show videos of products, and enable customers to make purchases. In-store promotions using QR codes can survey customer preferences and even involve customers in choice and design of future products.

Charity

See Non-Profits.

Classified Advertising

When using display classified ads—where you're allowed to use an image—place a QR code that leads to detailed online information (website, video, audio) about the item or service you're selling.

If your local newspaper allows QR codes in help wanted, place a QR code that links to the business website.

Clothing

Place QR codes on T-shirts and other clothing to help people immediately visit your website or send you a Twitter tweet. They can also go on sweatshirts, team jackets, scarves or hats. You can even integrate QR codes into the design of the fabric itself.

Clothing Manufacturers

QR codes on labels can link to cleaning instructions and locations where clothing is made. They can also link to catalogues and the ability to make purchases of additional clothing from the same manufacturer.

Club/Loyalty/Membership Cards

You can use your mobile phone's camera to take pictures of all your various club/membership cards—supermarket, health club, movie rental, big box discount store, pharmacy, and other chain retail outlets—and store them on your phone. When you're checking out of the supermarket or into a club, display the image of the club card on your phone. The checker can look at or scan the image, and you're in. Some phones have dedicated applications that will do all this and much more.

Colleges

Use QR codes on new student orientation literature to direct them to an orientation event calendar, interactive map of campus, map of the library, information on sports, clubs and other group activities, and social and academic events.

Here's a link to a Google map of the Stanford University campus:

Coffee Houses

No need for customer loyalty cards. Use QR codes instead. Customers can have their own QR ID codes stored in their phone's photo library that can be scanned at each purchase. Perhaps every tenth coffee is free. Or maybe let customers scan a QR code on each visit, and every 25th (or whatever) scan of the day wins a free coffee. Download cards can have QR codes for instant download of music track. QR codes displayed in-store can show where the day's coffee is grown, how it is processed, roasted and so on.

Comedians

Display QR codes at comedy club or on printed material to link to Facebook page, website, blog, access to CD catalog.

Comic Books

QR codes can link to comic book catalogue where readers can view past issues and other titles. Codes can also be integrated into the comic book story itself to provide extra information, reminders of past stories, hints and clues.

Commuter Services

QR codes on printed materials, at bus and train stops, and other locations can link to schedules, status, routes, and real-time arrivals and departures. Can also link to information on ride share programs, discount tickets and more.

Here's a link to BART (Bay Area Rapid Transit) in the San Francisco Bay Area:

Conference Badges

As on business cards, QR codes on conference badges can contain contact information. QR codes on badge or phone can serve as proof of registration. Exhibitors can scan badge QR codes to enter attendee in drawings, or for mailing product information after the conference. Attendees can scan each other's QR codes to get contact information for future use. Conference organizations can email QR codes linking to informational materials on the conference (maps, schedules, location information, speakers and their topics) so that attendees can have all necessary information on their phones.

Contact Information

QR codes can contain standard business card information. When scanned, most mobile phones will ask if you want the information to be added automatically to your phone's address book. Use contact information QR codes on business cards, brochures and other promotional material.

Here's typical contact information:

Contests

Phone users can enter contests simply by scanning a QR code to send an email or SMS message as their "entry form". You can announce contest winners via email or text messaging.

Cooking

Use QR codes in television commercials, on food packages or in newspaper or magazine food articles to link to recipes. Use them in cookbooks to link to recipe demonstration videos and other useful external information.

Counterfeit Protection

Scan the QR code on a product to see manufacturer, history and serial number information that must match the actual serial number on the product. For added security, the QR code can be on "scratcher" paper.

Coupons

Email QR code "coupons" that provide discounts or gifts for your loyal customers. Then scan the "coupon" image when a customer uses it to track the effectiveness of your marketing campaign.

Crime Prevention

QR codes in newspapers and on flyers can link to online crime reports by neighborhood, or to "Most Wanted "list with photos or videos of wanted persons. Another code can offer a direct link to a phone line other than 911 line for non-emergency contact with local police department.

Dating

Wear clothing or jewelry with QR codes that link to information about yourself that you're willing to share. Or keep the information to yourself, and only reveal the QR code to someone you're interested in.

Decals

Have decals made with your QR codes on them. Put them wherever you want people to see them. If you have a decal with a QR code for your contact information, you might want to be discreet where you put it. Place one on your mobile phone so that new acquaintances can easily scan it to get your contact information.

Direct Mail

In direct mail campaigns, place QR codes on all literature, so that prospects can link to websites, videos and audio files, coupons, or the opportunity to win a prize.

Directions

On maps, directories, signs and billboards place QR codes that link to navigation information that directs viewers to the chosen destination.

Door Hangers

Informational "hangers" left on the doorknobs of front doors are popular in the U.S. They're used by campaigning politicians as well as people offering services such as gardening and carpet cleaning. Don't just leave a hanger; leave a link to much more information on the Web. A QR code on the door hanger can link to more information, product and service reviews, prices, or a video message from the candidate or service provider.

Download Cards

Cards used by bands to promote their music have a URL that fans (and prospective fans) can use to download a free music track. Since music tracks can be played on mobile phones, make it easier for people and let them click on a QR code to automatically download the music straight to their phone. The codes work for ringtones as well.

But download cards don't need to be restricted to musicians. Any business could hand out cards with QR codes that let customers download information, calendars, discount coupons, and audio and video as well.

eBay Sales

1. To link to an item you're selling on eBay, simply copy the URL from the top of your browser when you're viewing the item, then paste that address into the URL field in a QR code generator. Here's what a typical eBay URL looks like:

http://cgi.ebay.com/NEW-Napa-Valley-Book-Winter-Mick-/400096434904?
cmd=ViewItem&pt=US_Nonfiction_Book&hash=item5d279b1ad8

The resulting QR code looks like this:

That's much too dense, so if you shorten the URL with a service such as bit.ly, the code then looks like this:

Education

QR codes provide the opportunity for teaching and learning to *expand* beyond the confines of a classroom. At lower levels they can be used for educational scavenger or treasure hunts. At middle levels, they can be used to connect students with more sophisticated information and to forums where they can discuss the subject matter with others. At higher levels, they can be used on course syllabi and printed handouts; to link to additional printed information such as full text print journals, as well as to websites, RSS feeds, or podcasts. QR codes are also very useful for directing students to information that becomes available after a syllabus has been printed by referring to a webpage that can be updated.

Email Notifications

Use QR codes to help people automatically sign up for contests, alerts, and mailing lists, or to join forums and other online groups.

Event Planners

Include a QR code on your event's print ads or flyers to let people register easily register for an event. At the same time people can enter contests held by the event. Eliminate check-ins by sending via email each registrant a QR code or software application prior to the event. Once they're at the event, they can use the application or have their QR code scanned at the door for instant check-in.

QR codes on registration badges let attendees scan the code to immediately download and retain a person's contact information. If each sponsor or exhibitor has a QR code prominently displayed at their exhibit, attendees can scan the code for more information at a later time or to bookmark a website for future visits. Use QR codes for scavenger hunts with gifts for those who successfully finish the hunt. Attended a session that you'd like more information on? Scan a prominently displayed QR code on the way out to have more information downloaded to your phone or to receive a transcript or Power Point presentation of the session you just attended.

See an interesting product at a booth? Booth staff can scan your personal QR code for contact information to send you information later, or you can scan the exhibit's QR code for later information acquisition on your own.

QR codes displayed throughout the event site can link you to information about nearby restaurants, parties, informal break out groups, points of interest, or other useful information. Attending an event in another country? QR codes can link you to all the information you need in your own language.

Are you an exhibitor who is frequently asked for your company's web address? Wear it on a T-shirt as a QR code that is labeled as such and can be easily scanned. Or wear a really big QR code button.

Facebook

Use QR codes to link to Facebook Pages. Just copy the URL for your page and use it to create a QR code. Put the code on business cards, your Facebook page, stickers or wherever else suits your fancy.

Here's a link to Lady Gaga's Facebook page:

Farmers Markets

QR codes displayed next to each type of produce can provide information on the type of vegetable, where it was grown and suggested recipes for its use.

Ferries

Use QR codes as commuter e-tickets. For tourists, have maps throughout the boat with QR codes that will link to audio narration describing sights along the way.

Here's a link to British Columbia Ferries in Canada:

Flyers

Use QR codes on flyers and notices on local bulletin boards. QR codes on a small 3" x 5" card can link to detailed information such as: For sale, wanted, help wanted, work wanted, services wanted and offered, events, local bands, lost and found pets, missing children,

Food

Use QR codes on food packaging to show ingredients and their source, nutritional value, recipes when relevant, and links to order forms and "Buy" buttons.

Foursquare

Use Foursquare (www.foursquare.com) to attract customers? Place a QR code somewhere that's obvious to your customers or clients, so that they can automatically check in to Foursquare through your location.

For example, here's a QR code that lets you instantly check in to Foursquare from the Powell Muni (public transport) Station in San Francisco.

You're currently at: Powell MUNI Station

Simply Scan Here to Instantly Check-In

Fundraisers

Use QR codes on promotional materials such as flyers and print ads. If the event includes silent or live auctions, post QR codes with each auction item that link to more information. For auction or raffle items such as airplane tickets and vacation stays, link to destination videos.

Games

Place QR codes on download cards, flyers, print ads or webpages so that readers can download mobile game applications directly to their phones.

Use QR codes for treasure hunts and scavenger hunts. At each point along the way, a new QR code can give further directions or clues.

Garage Sales / Yard Sales / Sidewalk Sales

Place QR codes on flyers that link to a list of key items—and photos if possible. Also use a QR code to link to a map showing the sale's location.

Gardening

QR codes on tags in the garden can provide information on watering as well as planting and expected harvest dates.

Geocaching

Use QR codes in geocaches and particularly as "travel bugs" . If you're not familiar with the GPS game of geocaching, you can find out all about it at www.geocaching.com.

Gifts

Both Zazzle (www.zazzle.com) and Café Press (www.cafepress.com) offer T-shirts and other clothing and paraphernalia that display custom QR codes. To see what's currently available, search for "QR code" at each of these websites. Cogteeth.com will let you make a customized QR code and then apply it to a Zazzle T-shirt, mug or card.

In fact, you can use your own custom QR code on any Zazzle or Cafe Press product. Just use one of the QR code generation sites listed in this book to create your QR code graphic, then use it at Zazzle or Cafe Press on your chosen product.

Get a set of mugs, each with a different QR code. Have your coffee drinking guests use their phones to scan the QR codes to see jokes or other humorous messages.

Gift Cards

Place a QR code on gift cards or reloadable debit cards from your business so that customers can scan the code to see their current balance. Using the phone's location-based capabilities, the code can also provide directions to the nearest store, or information on sales.

Governments

Local governments can use QR codes in a wide variety of ways. They can send out newsletters that contain QR codes to give citizens more information, including news and alerts. Post large QR codes at construction sites and other public works activities so citizens can scan the codes to learn about the project and its status. Encourage local businesses and tourist sites to use QR codes. Set up sightseeing walks with QR codes at signposts along the way.

One local government leading the way is the city of Manor, Texas. In Manor the codes are being used for a wide variety of purposes, including citizen communication, emergency management and at the town's historical sites. As the city's Manor Labs says on its website, "We conduct research and development on new, emerging technologies to better serve our residents. We work with numerous companies across the world to bring our residents cutting-edge technology and to help shape technology for other government agencies as well."

You can find out more at the city's website http://www.cityofmanor.org, and at http://www.manorlabs.org. You can also download a free document:

"White Paper: Redefining Government Communication with QR-Codes" at http://cityofmanor.org/comwhitepaper.pdf

Green

QR codes can save on paper. Instead of distributing documents each time they're updated, a constant QR code would link to ever-changing information so that people always have access to the very latest news and information.

Grocery Stores

At the entrance to the store and on every shopping cart, post QR codes that will download the day's specials to the customer's mobile phone. Another code will let customers download a detailed map of the store and its merchandise sections, or a special application that lets them search for an item and see its location.

Historic Sites

Use QR codes to provide text, audio and video information about the site. Use the codes inside buildings to provide specific information wherever appropriate. If a building is not accessible to public, use a QR code outside the building to link to a video tour of the building's interior.

Home

- Directions for visitors to your home (link to map)
- Pet tags
- Contents of stored boxes
- Games for children
- TV/movie schedules
- Online calendars of family members

ID Cards

QR codes on ID cards can match an online photo with the photo on the card to yield an additional security confirmation. Codes can also link to any additional information required.

Income

Wondering how you can generate income from QR codes? Read all the topics in this A to Z section, and you should be able to come up with a number of ideas.

Here are a few suggestions and reminders on how you can make money from QR codes themselves:

- Consulting
- Creation (not everyone wants to make QR codes themselves)
- Design and sell stickers, business cards, decals, bumper stickers, labels, T-shirts, baseball caps, iron-on patches for clothing, and temporary tattoos.
- Use with dating services
- Vending machine systems
- Traditional advertising media
- Jewelry
- As an advertising/marketing agency specializing in QR codes

Instant Winner

Phone users can scan QR codes to determine if they are instant winners. "Winners" can range from *everyone* to *every nth* user, such as every 50th scan receives a prize.

Instruction Manuals

QR code links to videos can show assembly, installation, use or repair of appliances, furniture, automobiles, toys, camping equipment and any other physical objects. If the manufacturer didn't do it, do it yourself.

Jewelry

QR codes, with the content of your choice, can be integrated into the design of many types of jewelry. While the Piaget piece shown might be within some budgets, chances are you might prefer something more simple and less costly.

Journalists and Reporters

Place a QR code containing your email address whenever possible along with a story or article you have written in a newspaper or magazine, or on the web. This will enable people to give you feedback as well as to send you leads for further stories.

Languages

QR codes on printed material or physical objects can link international users to information in their own language. They can also link students learning a language to additional material such as videos and websites in both their own language and their target language.

Here's a link to Google Translate, where you can translate text or entire webpages:

Libraries

Libraries are using QR codes in the results of a catalogue search, so patrons can save shelf locations on their mobile phone for easier book retrieval.

QR codes in library books can link dynamically to a book's due date and renewal phone number. They can also link to information about other books by the same author or by other authors that may be of interest to the reader, or to videos and websites of related interest.

QR codes in newsletters can link to reviews and other information on new acquisitions. They can also link to library hours and to the library's events calendar.

Scanning a QR code can directly download a library's ebook or podcast to a mobile phone. It can also connect a patron with the library's blog.

At journal and magazine shelves, QR codes can link a library patron to the online digital version of a printed publication

Some libraries are using QR codes to provide maps of the library and navigation directions, including virtual tours of the library, which helps patrons navigate through the various shelves and rooms. Others link patrons to the library's online booking system, where they can reserve a computer, a room, or audio visual equipment.

LinkedIn

Use QR codes wherever you wish to link people directly to your LinkedIn page.

Here's a code for a LinkedIn page:

Lodging

Hotels and resorts can use QR codes in all printed marketing materials. In-room QR codes can enable guests to download maps of the premises and surrounding area onto their mobile phones. Another code can let guests save the phone number of the hotel's front desk for quick calling from outside the premises.

Here's a link to a map of the Four Seasons Resort on the Big Island of Hawaii:

Lotteries

QR codes on flyers, posters, direct mail, and other printed material can let people enter a lottery by buying a (virtual) ticket through PayPal or another online payment system. Lottery winners can be announced via email or text messages.

Luggage

A QR code on your luggage tag can help to return your luggage to you when it gets lost. Because the code requires decoding, it is less easy for unscrupulous baggage handlers to note your home address while you're away on a trip.

Lyrics

QR Codes can link directly to song lyrics. Here's a link to the Beatles' "Happiness is a Warm Gun."

Magazines

Magazines can use QR codes in articles to provide additional or updated information. They can also take readers to online comments and forums. In print ads QR codes link to additional information on a product or service. With mobile payment, a reader can subscribe to the magazine by scanning a QR code, or buy a product mentioned or advertised in the magazine.

Mail / Package Delivery

Place a QR code on the outside of a package and notify the recipient in advance of delivery so that they can scan it upon arrival for confirmation as well as security purposes. Package carriers such as national post offices, FedEx and UPS already use various types of codes, including QR codes, to track packages along their route.

Manufacturers

A permanent QR code on an object can take the consumers to menus that list instruction manuals, warranties, troubleshooting, repairs, the opportunity to purchase replacement parts, and other useful information throughout the life of the product. At the very least, the code can link to the manufacturer's mobile-friendly website.

If the manufacturer doesn't do this, do it yourself. When you buy a new product that might need repair or troubleshooting in the future, go online and find the URL for the manual. Create a QR code for that URL, print it out and place it on the appliance yourself in case you need it in the future.

Maps

QR codes on printed maps can link to online interactive maps that cover the entire map area. Specific QR codes can link to major points of interest and transportation hubs. QR codes on urban maps can link to subway and bus routes, schedules and status.

This links to maps and other information for the London Tube:

Medication

QR codes on medication packaging and labels can link to important information about the medication that is large enough to actually be *readable*, including directions, ingredients, warnings, contraindications, and other essential information.

Meditation

Create QR codes that link to phone timer applications for timed meditations, or to audio recordings to lead one through guided meditations. This is an excellent way to pass the time when traveling or even just commuting by plane, bus or train..

Menus

QR codes on restaurant menus link to nutritional information on menu items, to sources of menu items—such as locally-grown vegetables, meats, and cheeses—to discount coupons for future meals at the restaurant, and to recipes.

Military

Scan QR codes to download manuals, rules and regulations, videos of protocol (such as saluting, placement of ribbons on dress uniforms), unit history, and more. QR codes can also be used on recruiting material to link to videos and other marketing material.

Here's a link to the PDF version of the Initial Entry Training Soldier's Handbook, which contains everything a US Army recruit will learn in basic training:

Mobile Games

Scan QR codes to download mobile games with automatic mobile payment, or as premiums from advertisers.

Movie Posters

QR codes on movie posters and other movie marketing materials can link to trailers for the movie, to reviews, or to a site where customers can buy tickets.

Museums

See Art Galleries and Zoos.

Music

Place QR codes on CD jewel cases so that people can order their own albums when they see one they like at a friend's. QR codes can link to online lyrics or even to sheet music, as well as to the band's/musician's website. QR codes can download music clips or entire MP3s.

MySpace

Create a QR code with the URL of your MySpace page to easily connect friends and other contacts to your page.

Here's a link to the MySpace page of Wyclef Jean:

Name Tags

Place QR codes on name tags at parties, conferences, or dating events to link people to appropriate online information such as their Facebook or LinkedIn page.

Napkins

If you manage a nightclub, bar, restaurant, airline or some other business that uses paper napkins for food or beverage service have a built-in medium for marketing. Include a QR code on your branded napkins. The code can link to anything you want to promote or to tell about your business, using audio, video, Facebook, Twitter, or your own website. You can provide links to coupons, menus, special events, branded clothing and souvenirs, music, discounted services, or anything else that will please your customers and benefit your business. You can even print up special napkins for your cocktail or barbeque guests with QR codes that link to jokes, photographs or other entertainment.

Neighborhoods

Murmur (www.murmurtoronto.ca) is a project that began in Toronto, Ontario and has spread to many other locations. It initially used phone numbers to let people in a neighborhood learn about the neighborhood, its history and its residents through audio recordings made by current or past neighbors. Murmur then began to use SMS messages instead of phone calls. QR codes would be even more effective. (See also Yellow Arrow)

Newspapers

Print regular sidebars reminding readers how they can turn their mobile phones into QR code scanners. QR codes in the news and feature sections of your newspaper can enable readers to see earlier stories, expanded versions of current stories, and related or breaking news on articles that they just read. When products, books, or services are reviewed or discussed in feature articles, a QR code at the end of an article can link to ways for readers to immediately buy the item that they just read about, earning affiliate commissions for your newspaper. Or the QR codes can link to local stores that have paid for the link, showing a map of the store's location.

Articles in the entertainment section can contain QR codes that let the reader buy movie or concert tickets, possibly with another commission going to your newspaper. The same is true for travel articles, letting people immediately book a flight or cruise. Articles can include QR code links to promotional videos, movie trailers, travel videos, and sports events.

In advertisements, newspaper readers can learn more about products or services, and even hear recordings or see videos. Advertisers get great benefits, too. Through web analytics, advertisers can see exactly how much active interest there is in their products and build up a mailing list to offer related product information.

Because the QR code passes through the paper's website before going to the advertiser, the newspaper can, if it wishes, collect a per click charge as well as a display ad fee. Ad prices could be negotiated with lower rate for print ads that are accompanied by PPC (Pay Per Click) charge. However, make sure there's no charge to the advertiser for your creation and tracking of the QR codes, and use this service simply as a come-on to businesses to advertise in your paper.

Make sure you use QR codes in your house ads, particularly when you're promoting your own mobile website. While you're at it, link to your paper's Twitter and Facebook accounts as well.

In food sections, the codes can enable your readers to download recipes and lists of ingredients they'll need to make a dish. Restaurant reviews can have QR codes linking directly to a restaurant's website and map location, its menu, and even to a site where they can make an online reservation.

Comic pages can have QR codes linking to past comics and the opportunity to buy original comics by the same artist.

Sports pages can link to a wide variety of websites with text articles, audio and videos so that the entire sports world comes alive on the reader's phone. In some cases, the QR codes can even link to live streaming video of sports events.

On editorial and opinion pages, readers can use QR codes to immediately make comments, submit letters to the editor, or join discussion forums.

Restaurants, stores and other businesses can offer coupons with special prices for the day or week. SMS numbers can also be included along with the QR codes so that those readers without more up-to-date phones don't feel penalized.

And of course anytime a newspaper promotes its mobile features, it should include a QR code that links to its mobile site, such as this one for the *San Francisco Chronicle*:

Nightclubs

Place QR codes on newsletters and flyers, and in print ads that link to schedules of upcoming performers and to online ticket purchasing. Tickets can be paperless, using QR codes so that club personnel can simply scan your phone's screen to see that you have a valid ticket.

Non-Profits

Place QR codes on solicitation mail, and on your organization's brochures and other literature, so that people can make an instant donation using their mobile phone. QR codes can also help them to sign up for events or to volunteer.

Here's a video on their use in Vancouver, Canada for easy donating to charity.

http://bit.ly/hhupPr

At a surfing competition in the U.S., the Oral Cancer Foundation gave away QR code tattoo transfers and T-shirts to publicize the dangers of oral cancer.

Nurseries

Nurseries can use QR codes to provide detailed information about plants so that customers can learn about sun and shade requirements, seasonality and climate needs, watering instructions, dealing with insects and other pests, medicinal or nutritional value, and other important information.

Office

- Track documents
- Label contents of storage boxes
- Create a staff home phone directory
- Make product lists
- Provide equipment troubleshooting and repair

Outdoor Advertising

For safety reasons, QR codes should be used only on outdoor advertising that is aimed at pedestrians, not automobile drivers. Since billboards, lighting and other outdoor displays are location-specific, where possible take advantage of the location and its amenities to highlight the advantages of your product. Don't just place a huge QR code outdoors; give some hint as to why passers-by should scan it with their phones.

Parking

Have a QR code at each parking place in a garage or lot. Drivers can scan the code to download a description of the location and even a map. This will help them find their way in the area as well as return to their car.

Parks

QR codes can be used in public parks and botanical gardens to provide information about landmarks, statues and artwork, directions to restrooms, and identification of trees, flowers and even wildlife—though the wildlife code will likely need to be in a fixed location rather than attached to a local squirrel.

PayPal

Use QR codes linked to PayPal or other online payment systems for immediate purchase of items, to make donations, or to initiate a paid subscription to your publication or service.

This code will link you to PayPal's mobile site:

Personal Use

- Create a QR code with your contact information and save it in the photo section of your phone. When someone wants your contact information, they can simply scan the photo displayed on your phone's screen.

- Use codes as IDs on books, purses and phones

- Design your own t-shirts, earrings, rings, clothing patches, or his and her gifts

- Place codes on your websites

- Use codes on, or to link to, your accounts on Facebook, MySpace, Twitter, LinkedIn and other social media sites

Pet Stores

Display QR codes linking to websites for your local humane society so that customers can see Lost Pets, Found Pets, and Pets for Adoption. Other codes can link to assembly instructions for elaborate pet play structures, to videos of animals playing with toys, or how-to videos on grooming, nail cutting and other skills for pet owners.

Pets

A QR code on a pet collar tag can help a lost pet get home. The finder can scan the code and see the pet's name, and the phone number, email address and other contact information for the owner or the pet's veterinarian.

Phone Calls

For young children or people with certain disabilities, it's easier to scan a QR code containing a telephone number than to key in a phone number.

Picnic and Rest Sites

QR codes at picnic or rest stops along highways can provide useful information such as landmarks viewed from the site, or weather forecasts, traffic conditions, and emergency information.

Podcasting

QR codes can contain URLs so that the user can bookmark or subscribe to a podcast series, or immediately download a podcast.

Here's a link to a wonderfully touching podcast from Radiolab in New York City entitled "Bus Stop" about a solution for wandering nursing home patients with Alzheimer's and Dementia.

Politicians

Politicians who include a QR code on brochures, newsletters, flyers, signs and billboards can provide links directly to their websites or to a video or audio message. Codes can also let constituents easily phone or send email to the politician's office.

Postcards

Use QR codes along with regular marketing or other text on postcards so that the reader can easily scan the code and go to a website containing much more detailed information.

Posters

QR codes can enhance almost any type of poster by providing links to more detailed information or even purchase options.

Presentations

Making a presentation with PowerPoint or another type of presentation tool? Place a couple of QR codes on the final image of your presentation so that members of your audience can scan the code to get a copy of your presentation; link to additional related information; or download your contact information to their phones.

Programs

QR codes inside programs for theatrical or musical events, lectures, and other types of performances can link to additional text information, videos (such as demonstrations of types of dance or musical works), audio commentary by a playwright, actor or composer, and even link to online forums where the user can join in on a discussion of the event. As an income source for both the performer and the theater, QR codes can link to sites where the reader can buy CDs, DVDs or books.

Puzzles

QR codes make great jigsaw puzzles. Small puzzles make excellent promotional gifts with the completed QR code leading to a prize or purchase option.

Radio Stations

QR codes displayed in print ads or on a radio station's website can link to the station's webpage and program schedule.

Raffles

Clicking on a QR code can enable people to automatically buy a raffle ticket using PayPal or other online payment system. The sponsor can announce winners via email or text message.

Real Estate

QR codes in newspaper and magazine ads, in real estate publications, and on signs at the properties for sale can link to detailed information including floor plans, statistics, and narrated video tours of the exterior and interior of the property.

Religious Organizations

QR codes can link from printed or email newsletters, or newspaper announcements to music, activity schedules, and pre-recorded sermons.

Resorts

Newspaper and magazine ads can contain QR codes that link to high quality videos promoting the resort and all its features. The codes can even offer online booking for vacation stays.

Here's a link to a video on Disney's Caribbean Beach Resort:

Restaurants

QR codes on restaurant menus can lead to interesting details on the food item and its history. They can also provide information on, and the sources of ingredients, nutritional information, and recipes—when the restaurant is willing to divulge them. Perhaps restaurants may also want to use a special QR code that offers a free dessert or some other sort of reward on every 25th scan.

Ringtones

QR codes can lead directly to paid or free ringtones.

RSS Feeds

QR codes on websites or on printed material, or sent through email or e-newsletters can link to a particular RSS feed for a blog or website.

Here's a link to the RSS feed for ESPN's Sports Headlines:

Rubber Stamps

Order a self-inking rubber stamp made to print a QR code that links to your website. You'll have an instantly-usable QR code imprinter that you can use anywhere you find an appropriate flat surface.

Scavenger Hunts

Both adults and children can follow QR codes from place to place on a scavenger-type hunt. Each QR code would contain a hint that sends them to a new location. The first group to collect the appropriate objects, visit every one of the designated locations, or arrive at the final destination is the winner.

Secrets

You can use QR codes to send secret messages that can be decoded by your friends. The text in a QR code can itself already be encoded so that even if someone else scans the QR code they won't be able to read the message unless they also have the original text code.

Security

QR codes can be used for document verification, such as ID cards and certificates. A QR code on the document can link to a photo of the registered owner or subject of the document. Codes can confirm purchase of an item, or of legitimate admission to a secure area, an event or a planes or train.

Self-guided Tours

(See Tours)

Semapedia

Semapedia's goal is "to connect the virtual and physical world by bringing the right information from the internet to the relevant place in physical space."

To do this, it invites people (you) to come to their website and make "Semapedia-Tags". These tags are QR codes that can contain only web addresses. You can print these tags on stickers or labels and paste them everywhere in your physical world. When people see the tag, they'll be able to scan it with their mobile phone and go to the website whose address you encoded into the tag.

The catch? Only one. The only address you can enter into a Semapedia-Tag is one that leads to one of the public domain, non-profit, community-built "Wiki" addresses, which include the original free online encyclopedia "Wikipedia" (www.wikipedia.org), and any of Wikipedia's sister projects such as Wikibooks, Wikinews, and Wikisource.

The reason you're limited to these web addresses is that the project's goal is to link the "Wiki" information, which is entirely and collaboratively entered by volunteers (this also can mean *you*), to all places in the real, physical world to which it is relevant. The Semapedia volunteers believe it's important to bring knowledge to the place where it matters, making it accessible in order to change minds and worlds.

Note: All web links first go to Semapedia's own site before linking to the appropriate Wiki page. This is to ensure that all QR codes are directed to a *mobile* version of the Wiki website, so that the resulting information is properly displayed on a mobile phone.

You can create your own Semapedia-Tags at the project's home page, http://en.semapedia.org/.

Sex

We might as well admit that Sex Sells. It was a prime engine behind the growth of VHS, DVDs, and even the Web, so we'll likely see the same with QR codes. We'll leave it up to you if you wish to use the concept for fun, profit or not at all, but if you're interested, here's someone's very soft core start.

Sheet Music

QR codes on sheet music can link directly to an audio recording of the music, or to instructions and tips on playing the musical piece.

For example, here's a link to the sheet music for Erik Satie's *"3 Gymnopedies No. 1."*

SMS Alerts

QR codes containing an SMS (Short Message Service) number give a   user the chance to sign up directly for future text alerts from the SMS service.

For example, Google's SMS service lets you send a query for a wide variety of information. If you scan the following QR code, you will enter the SMS address **466453** ("GOOGLE"). Then type "weather [your city]". Google will return a weather forecast. (For a list of all options, just send the text "help".

Sign-ups

QR codes can contain email or SMS addresses or, if appropriate, message text that enables the user to sign up for alerts, email lists, e-newsletters, and other digital subscriptions.

Skiing

QR codes at rest stops, restaurants and gas stations on the way to ski resorts can give skiers real-time ski and road conditions in the mountains ahead. The codes can link to weather forecasts, snow pack, wind speeds, temperatures and web cams.

Here's a link to conditions at Whistler Blackcomb in British Columbia, Canada.

Social Media

Social Media are a natural for the use of QR codes, particularly since all major social media websites have mobile phone applications. For specifics, see Facebook—page 69, LinkedIn—page 76, MySpace—page 80, and

Twitter—page 99. Keep in mind that you can create QR codes for the URL of your websites on any other social media as well.

Sporting Events

QR codes can link to schedules for sporting events, can download audio or video recordings, or even provide real-time streaming.

Sporting Goods

QR codes on or near products in sporting goods stores can use video to demonstrate the use of the items. Customers can download digital information on top athletes, and video or audio by or about those athletes.

Stickers

You can place stickers with QR codes containing your contact information in books and on other items you wish to have returned if lost.

Stock Cars

Got a race car? Don't just put logos on the car; put a QR code on each side of the car linking to your website.

Stores

Place QR codes on or near products so that customers can see reviews and examples of how they are used. In your storefront windows, place QR codes next to each item, so that people outside the store, particularly during hours when the store is closed, can use their phones to link to information about the items in the window.

Next to selected items *inside* the store, you can place QR codes that link to detailed information—particularly videos—about the featured items.

Students

Younger students can follow, and make up their own, QR codes for scavenger hunt-type games. They can also link to appropriate websites and to websites designed by the students themselves. The codes can also be used for tours, or to link to relevant information at class outings, school exhibits and science fairs. Older students can insert QR codes into their artwork, science projects, and any other form of presentation.

Students in higher level or college can receive syllabi and assignment sheets that include QR codes for links to online resources, and to new and updated information. Students of all ages can add QR codes to their reports or papers to link to relevant external information, including websites, audio and video.

Tattoos

Temporary (or, yes, even permanent) tattoos can use QR codes as the design. Have a permanent tattoo of your lover's name, but you've since split up and acquired a new true love? What if instead you had used a QR code linked to a website about the old girl (or boy) friend? Instead of removing the tattoo, all you would have needed to do is change the text and photos on the website.

Taxis

Place QR codes on signs visible from the outside of bars and restaurants. After patrons leave the establishment and decide they need a taxi, they can scan the QR code on the sign and immediately have the taxi company's phone number inserted into their dialer.

Teachers

Integrating large QR codes into PowerPoint and other presentations allows students to scan and download relevant information and save you the effort and cost of printing hardcopy handouts. (See also the Students listing for more ideas).

A class roster with a QR code for each student (you'll have to create this yourself) can link you to the Facebook or MySpace page for the many students who have them. This may give you information that helps you deal with behavioral or learning problems if they occur.

Using QR codes instead of student names on test papers can assure confidentiality and anonymity and eliminate any possible biases, pro or con.

Teams

Place QR codes on team jackets, sweatshirts, T-shirts and other clothing so that fans can immediately link to the team's website or Facebook page, or send a Tweet. Use also to link fans to online sites where they can buy clothing and merchandise bearing the team's logo. Game programs can have QR codes for more information, audio and video on the team, its history, and its individual players and, of course, for sales of team merchandise.

Theme Parks

If QR codes are visible throughout the park, they can offer discounts on restaurant meals and souvenirs, prizes, or discounted tickets for future visits. They might also allow visitors to download a full park map, or a map to restrooms, or event schedules. How about historical or behind-the-scenes information on points of interest, including audio and video? Park management can also use park-created QR codes as virtual credit cards which, when scanned, enable the phone's owner to pay for items and services.

Here's the mobile website for Walt Disney World in Florida:

Tickets

You can purchase tickets in advance and get a unique just-for-you QR coded ticket delivered to your phone via SMS or email. When you enter the event, the ticket taker will scan your phone's screen and you'll be admitted. For a low-cost, mobile-based ticketing service, see www.wikkit.com.

Tombstones

It's starting to happen now in Japan. Tombstones can contain a QR code which, when scanned, takes you to a website with information about, and even a video of, the deceased.

Tours

QR codes can lead people on a self-guided tour. The codes can appear on a printed map or directory, or on signs along the route. They'll provide information on a location, including text, audio, video, virtual tours of the inside of buildings, old photographs and other historical information including dramatic re-creations of events at the location, as well as directions to the next stop on the tour.

Tourism

QR codes can be used in countless ways, including right on site at historic and interesting locations, or on brochures and maps. The State of Arkansas Tourism Division is using QR codes as shortcuts to link to various pages on its website so that visitors can see maps and ideas for scenic driving routes.

For example, this QR code links directly to daily updates on the best locations to see fall foliage.

Toys

QR codes on toys can link to step-by-step assembly videos, information on similar or associated products for sale, or entertaining videos starring the toys themselves.

Traffic Reports

QR codes at highway rest areas, roadside restaurants, gas stations and other locations on travelers' routes can link drivers to real-time traffic information. The codes can even link to webcams for viewing of the actual conditions.

This links to the mobile site for 511.org which provides real-time traffic information for the entire San Francisco Bay Area.

Trains

Trains can use QR codes on printed material, in stations, and even on board the trains themselves. Travelers can use the codes to access schedules, current status, and scenic information and points of interest along the train's route.

Here's the link to the mobile website for the US rail system Amtrak:

Travel Advertising

Print advertising comes alive through QR codes when they link to videos showing things to do at the traveler's destinations, or a video experience of life on a cruise ship.

Here's a video showing life for first-time cruisers on a Carnival Cruise Line ship:

Treasure Hunts

Use QR codes for kids (or adults) treasure hunts. Each QR code leads through hints or GPS locations to the next QR code, until the game players finally arrive at the final destination, where they win, or automatically receive, a prize.

Television Stations

Show QR codes for the station itself pointing out that viewers can scan them and bookmark the station's schedule website on their phone. Can also be used to access information on specific TV programs and actors. Stations can also use QR codes in conjunction with television commercials, giving the station the unique ability to track audience response to the commercials.

Stations can also set up QR codes so that they will provide calendar alerts to viewers for specific programs.

Here's a mobile site for a television station in Madison, Wisconsin:

Twitter

Use QR codes to automatically link to personal or business accounts allowing people to see your tweets or to follow you, or to see hashtags (#xxx) for relevant subjects. A QR code can also let a phone owner send a tweet to his or her account.

#qrcodes   **Scan Me's Twitter page**

Using Paper.li (www.paper.li), you can also set up a QR code to link to the virtual newspaper you've created on a particular topic. Here's one to the #qrcodes Daily:

Vehicles

Laminated car magnets with QR codes on vehicles let people scan the code for information on the organization or company.

Vending Machines

Japanese vending machines may become a model for vending machines everywhere. To use them simply scan the QR code for the product you want. Your order will be placed, your account will be billed, and the item will be delivered immediately by the machine.

The same principle will work with any type of purchase under any conditions, including access to entertainment, sports events, museums or transportation. All that's needed is a QR code on or near the product (or entrance), and an appropriate payment plan set up previously. This could also be done with paper bills received in the mail, or electronic billing received via email.

Wallpaper

QR codes on TV, in print, or on posters and billboards will enable phone users to download wallpaper images to their phones automatically.

Wearables

QR codes can be worn as T-shirts and other clothing, as designs on jewelry, or even as temporary, or permanent, tattoos.

Weather Reports

Whether you're at home or traveling, QR codes in prominent public places can link you to the latest weather reports.

This code links to Weather.com, which offers weather reports for many locations:

Webcams

QR codes linking to webcams serve a variety of purposes such as weather and traffic conditions, beach crowds, surf conditions, and snow levels.

Here's a live webcam in Phuket, Thailand:

Website Designers

Place a QR code on the desktop version of your site so that visitors can easily bookmark the mobile version of your site.

Wedding Planners

Prior to the wedding, guests can receive a QR code linking to a map and directions to the wedding and reception locations. If nicely done, it could even be printed on the invitation, or at least as a supplement in the invitation package. Planners might also email the code to invitees who respond that they will be attending the wedding.

Wineries/Wine Labels

Use QR codes for self-guided tours at the actual winery, with either audio or video recordings at key locations on the tour. Place QR codes on back labels so that customers can find out more about the wine, its source vineyards, the winemaker, aging, recommended foods, reviews and any other useful or promotional information. Or use the label's QR code to go to a video tour of the winery.

Yellow Arrow

Yellow Arrow is—or at least *was*—a public art project initiated in New York City. Their website at www.yellowarrow.net is still on display but as of this writing has not been updated for a long time. When the project was still functioning, you could download yellow arrow stickers to print and place anywhere in public spaces (assuming local authorities didn't mind too much.)

On the yellow sticker would be a link connecting to a particular phone number. Shortly after, you would receive a return text message left by the sticker's original owner.

The Yellow Arrow symbol means "There's more here: a hidden detail, a funny story, a memory, or a crazy experience." Each arrow links digital content to the arrow's location using a mobile phone.

While Yellow Arrow initially used SMS messages for communicating and required that the host maintain telephone service, a similar art project could now be done with QR codes that link to a website which in turn would display text, audio, photos or video—all linked in relevance to that arrow's specific location.

Yelp

QR codes can link to reviews on Yelp and other review sites for restaurants, shops, and other businesses. Of course you as a proprietor will want to do this only if the reviews are positive.

Here's a link to Yelp's mobile site:

And here's a link to the Yelp entry and reviews for Pearl Restaurant in Napa, California:

YouTube

This code links to YouTube's main mobile site at http://m.youtube.com.

To create a QR code for a specific YouTube video, simply copy the URL, shorten it with a service such as bit.ly, and then use a QR code generator to create the final QR code.

Zoos

QR codes at zoo entrances can link to a map of the zoo which the visitor can download. At each different animal location in the zoo, a QR code may provide audio narration, or even a video, giving detailed information about the animal. There can be specific QR codes for specific international languages.

This code links to a welcome video featuring John Cleese at the Santa Barbara Zoo:

Other QR codes at the Santa Barbara Zoo link to a variety of information on animals throughout the zoo.

Appendix A – Other Types of Barcodes

In the main section of this book, we mentioned the original type of code, which is the one-dimensional (1d) barcode. These are still primarily used for manufacturing and publishing purposes. But there are a number of 2d codes which look similar to QR codes and can be used for the same purposes. Sometimes they have features which are more useful than QR codes. Be aware, however, that most of these codes are proprietary. The inventor owns the patents, controls their use, and licenses their use to you. This is often at no cost to you, but there are usually strings attached. We'll talk about those strings later.

First, however, let's go back to the original one-dimensional barcodes and how you can read them with your QR code reader.

1D Barcodes

UPC (UCC)

UPS barcodes, now officially known as UCC barcodes, are the most common and have been around on products for years. They look like this:

ISBN

The International Standard Book Number (ISBN) is a unique numeric commercial book identifier. An ISBN is assigned to each edition and version (but not reprintings) of a book. The ISBN is 13 digits long if assigned after January 1, 2007, and 10 digits long if assigned before 2007. The USBN is one type of EAN-13 code (see following section).

An ISBN consists of 4 or 5 parts. Most of these parts are used by other types of UCC barcodes as well.

1. For a 13 digit ISBN, a GS1 prefix: 978 or 979 (indicating the industry; in this case, 978 denotes book publishing)

2. The group identifier (language-sharing country group)

3. The publisher code

4. The item number (title of the book)

5. A checksum character or check digit (for error checking)

The ISBN separates its parts (group, publisher, title and check digit) with either a hyphen or a space.

Group Identifier

The group identifier is a one to five digit number. As examples, the single digit group identifiers are: 0 or 1 for English-speaking countries, 2 for French-speaking countries, 3 for German-speaking countries, 4 for Japan, 5 for Russian-speaking countries, 7 for People's Republic of China, 957+986 for Republic of China, and 962+988 for Hong Kong. In the symbol shown above, the 81 indicates India.

Prefixes (for all types of goods)

- 0, 1, 6, 7, 8: For most products.
- 2: Reserved for local use (store/warehouse), for items sold by variable weight. Variable-weight items, such as meats and fresh fruits

and vegetables, are assigned a UPC by the store, if they are packaged there.

- 3: Drugs by National Drug Code number.
- 4: Reserved for local use (store/warehouse), often for loyalty cards or store coupons.
- 5: Coupons
- 9: Coupons

EAN-13

EAN-13 (European Article Number) barcode, now officially referred to as International Article Number although it retains the same abbreviation. The barcode is used worldwide for marking products often sold at retail. The encoded numbers are *product identification numbers*, which are also called Japanese Article Number in Japan.

All the numbers in UPC/UCC and EAN barcodes are known as "Global Trade Item Numbers (GTIN)".

Scanning 1d Barcodes

Most QR code (2d) reader applications will also read the original 1d barcode, such as this one:

Since barcodes are used on most products, the information they contain—or point to through the use of their encoded number—can be very useful.

UPC Database

www.upcdatabase.com

This website has a large database of UPC (Universal Product Codes) codes (more than 1.3 million entries when we last checked.) It includes UPC codes (more precisely these days referred to as UCC-12 codes for "Uniform Code Council"), as well as UCC-13 and EAN-13, which are commonly used for books.

At the UPC Database website, use the small Actions menu on the left to go to "Look Up." Then enter a barcode number in the "Item Lookup" field, making sure you use no spaces or hyphens.

If the product is listed, you will probably see an illustration and available prices, as well as detailed information.

Item Lookup

www.itemlookup.net

Another useful site. Look up ISBN (10 or 13 digit numbers), UPC/UCC (12 digit numbers) and EAN (13 digit numbers). If the product is listed, you will probably see an illustration as well as detailed information and links to Amazon information, prices and reviews.

Create your own 1d barcodes

www.barcoding.com/upc/

If you'd like to create your own barcode, using such formats as UPC, UCC or EAN, go to Barcoding Inc. They'll be happy to sell you barcode software, printers and scanners, but they also let you make your own barcode images online at no charge.

Comparative Shopping

By scanning a product's barcode, or entering its barcode number, you can get information on prices at online and local merchants. Here are some popular applications, and the phones with which they work at the time of writing.

Google Shopper

www.google.com/mobile/shopper/

Scan a barcode, search by voice (just say the product name), or point your phone's camera at the cover art of a book, CD, DVD, or video game. Results include detailed product information, reviews and prices. Save history and favorite scans, and share them with friends. *Android.*

NexTag Mobile

www.nextag.com/

Compare prices on products from thousands of online merchants. Scan the barcode or type in the barcode number to see prices, reviews, ratings and descriptions. *Android, iPhone, Blackberry.*

Red Laser

www.redlaser.com/

Scan the barcode or enter the barcode number. See local and online prices, find books at local libraries in the U.S., see nutritional labels, and check foods against a list of common allergens. Red Laser now scans QR codes as well. *iPhone.*

Shop Savvy Barcode Scanner

www.biggu.com/

Scan items for prices both online and at local retailers. Current focus is on higher end items including books, DVDs and video games, consumer electronics, and soft goods, groceries, health and beauty items. Features include reviews, price alerts, and a history of your scans. *Android, iPhone, Nokia.*

Other 2D Barcodes

The two most commonly used 2d codes are QR Codes and Datamatrix codes. Most of the others are proprietary, owned and controlled by the companies that created them. Some have been made available for anyone to use. Because QR codes are always larger than Datamatrix codes (usually about 60% larger), the smaller Datamatrix codes are primarily used in manufacturing, production and inventory control. But for personal use, and use with the general public, the QR codes are excellent and the most commonly used.

While there are special pieces of sophisticated equipment you can buy that will read QR codes, particularly codes containing large amounts of data—Denso itself sells such equipment—purchasing them makes no sense for the average user. Anyone with a camera-equipped mobile phone can read QR codes. The QR code scanning software is available at no charge for all commonly-used Internet mobile phones.

Aztec Code

Aztec Code was invented in 1995, has been used commercially since 1997, and is now in the public domain. It reportedly displays well on mobile devices, and as a result it's used for tickets by various railway systems in Europe.

http://en.wikipedia.org/wiki/Aztec_Code
http://www.terryburton.co.uk/barcodewriter/generator/

BeeTagg

www.beetagg.com

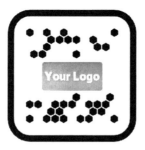

BeeTagg is a Swiss company that states that its symbol is designed specifically for mobile tagging and particularly for uses that require a security layer, such as tickets, coupons and voting. BeeTagg also lets you place a small logo within the center of the symbol.

Although BeeTagg is patented, anyone can create BeeTagg 2d codes. BeeTagg's free online code generator creates codes for BeeTagg, QR and Datamatrix codes. To use it, go to http://generator.beetagg.com. You can also generate any of the three codes to produce a code specifically designed for Facebook, YouTube, eBay, or the RSS feed in a blog. In addition, BeeTagg's *Multicode Manager* lets you track campaigns and applications using any of the three 2d codes. Their *Publishers, Agency* and *Brand Editions* offer more sophisticated and specific features for those commercial ventures.

NOTE:

> When you use BeeTagg's free version, you are subject to this caution from the company: "We reserve the right to display a BeeTagg Welcome Page (with or without ads) before the user accesses the actual content. This will happen not every time, but randomly."

BeeTagg also offers a free multicode reader at their website. It reads their own proprietary code as well as QR and Datamatrix codes. At the time of this writing, the reader supported a wide variety of phones, including iPhone, Android, Blackberry, HTC, LG, Mio, Motorola, Nokia, Palm, Samsung, Siemens, SonyEriccson, and SPV.

Datamatrix

The *Datamatrix* code is similar to a QR code and best used on small objects. It is a two-dimensional matrix barcode consisting of black and white "cells" or modules arranged in either a square or rectangular pattern. The information to be encoded can be text or raw data. The usual data size is from a few bytes up to two kilobytes. Error correction codes are added to increase symbol strength: even if they are partially damaged, they can still be read. A Datamatrix symbol can store up to 2,335 alphanumeric characters.

Every Datamatrix is composed of two solid adjacent borders in an "L" shape (called the "finder pattern") and two other borders consisting of alternating dark and light "cells" or modules (called the "timing pattern"). Within these borders are rows and columns of cells encoding information. The finder pattern is used to locate and orient the symbol while the timing pattern provides a count of the number of rows and columns in the symbol. As more data is encoded in the symbol, the number of cells (rows and columns) will increase. The symbol sizes vary from 8×8 to 144×144.

The most popular application for Datamatrix is to mark small items. A Datamatrix can encode fifty characters in a symbol that is readable at two or three mm^2 and be read with only a 20 percent contrast ratio. The Datamatrix is scalable, with commercial applications as small as 300 micrometers (laser etched on a 600 micrometer silicon device) and as large as a one meter (3 feet) square (painted on the roof of a boxcar). Fidelity of the marking and reading systems are the only limitation.

The Electronic Industries Alliance recommends using Datamatrix for labeling small electronic components, and the American military and aerospace industry use Datamatrix extensively.

Datamatrix was invented by International Data Matrix, Inc. It is now in the public domain for many applications, which means it can be used free of any licensing or royalties.

Free online Datamatrix generators are at:

> http://datamatrix.kaywa.com/
> http://www.i-nigma.com/CreateBarcodes.html

High Capacity Color Barcode
(see Microsoft Tag, page 114)

Microglyph/Dataglyph
www.microglyphs.com

Microglyph is the exclusive worldwide licensee of DataGlyphs, developed by Xerox PARC, the Xerox Corporation's Palo Alto Research Center, in the 1990s, primarily for document handling.

[The following is from Xerox' website at:
http://www.xerox.com/Static_HTML/xsis/dataglph.htm]

> They encoded information into thousands of tiny, individual glyph elements. Each element consisted of a small 45 degree diagonal line, as short as 1/100th of an inch or less, depending on the resolution of the printing and scanning that was used. Each one represented a single binary 0 or 1, depending on whether it sloped

to the left or right. Sequences of these could be used to encode numeric, textual or other information.

The individual glyphs were grouped together on the page, where they formed unobtrusive, evenly textured gray areas, like half-toned pictures. One of the reasons for using diagonal glyph elements was because research showed that the patterns that they formed when massed together were not visually distracting.

DataGlyph technology allowed ordinary business documents to carry thousands of characters of information hidden in these unobtrusive gray patterns that could appear as backgrounds, shading patterns or conventional graphic design elements. They could be shaped as logos to embedded into a picture. Often, their presence would go completely unnoticed. (The entire Gettysburg Address would fit in a DataGlyph about the size of a small US postage stamp.)

Photos courtesy of PARC - Palo Alto Research Center Incorporated © 2010 PARC

Microglyphs are very flexible and can be applied to surfaces that are reflective or curved (such as batteries and tire sidewalls), can take arbitrary shapes and integrate unobtrusively with logos or images into such items as smart cards, and used for counterfeit protection. They have adjustable error correction and are compatible with cryptography. Common applications include document management, fraud prevention, inventory tracking, ID cards, parts marking and product tagging.

www.xerox.com/Static_HTML/xsis/dataglph.htm

For comments from the inventor:

www.tauzero.com/Rob_Tow/DataGlyph.html

Microsoft Tag

www.microsoft.com/tag

[imagine this in color]

Microsoft Tag is the product using High Capacity Color Barcode (HCCB) technology. HCCB is the name coined by Microsoft for its proprietary technology of encoding data in a 2D "barcode" using clusters of colored triangles instead of the square pixels traditionally associated with 2D barcodes.

Microsoft Tags are totally outside established standards in the industry. The plus side is that they are colorful, using patterns of cyan, magenta, yellow and black with white lines. They're designed to work with mobile phone cameras under less than desirable conditions: low resolution, low light performance, and slow shutter speed.

Microsoft's special *Tag Reader* does the same job as ordinary QR Code Readers do with QR and other codes. One difference is that codes can never lead directly to your own website. The Tag Reader decodes the symbol, sends the decoded content to Microsoft's servers, and then Microsoft's servers tell your phone what to do. The reader is available for all standard camera-equipped smartphones.

PDF417

PDF417 is a stacked linear 2d barcode symbol format used in a variety of applications, primarily transportation, identification cards, and inventory management. The PDF417 format is in the public domain. This is the type of code now being used by Starbucks for mobile payments.

www.tec-it.com/online-demos/tbarcode/barcode-generator.aspx

Semacode

www.semacode.com

Semacode uses the Datamatrix format for its 2d codes. Their reader for the iPhone supports both Datamatrix and QR codes. The company's website states that Semacode tags are an "open system" and that tag creation is "completely unrestricted,"

Create Semacode tags

www.invx.com

This website lets you enter text and simultaneously generate QR and Semacode or Datamatrix symbols.

ShotCode

www.shotcode.org

ShotCode is a circular barcode created by High Energy Magic of Cambridge University. It uses a dartboard-like circle, with a bulls-eye in the center and data circles surrounding it. The technology reads data bits from these data circles by measuring the angle and distance from the bulls-eye for each.

ShotCodes do not contain regular data but instead store a lookup number. When a ShotCode is scanned, your phone's browser will first connect with the ShotCode website, which will then re-direct your browser to the intended URL.

SPARQCode

www.sparqcode.com

SPARQCodes are based on the standard QR code. Although SPARQCodes are trademarked, there is no license required to use them. To create a SPARQCode at no charge, go to www.sparqcode.com/static/maestro. Be aware that, when scanned, any code you create will first pass through the sparqcode.com website before completing your intended action.

The company states that the codes can be read by most standard QR code readers. The company's focus is on providing auxiliary services such as barcode generation, payments, web integration, analytics, trivia and contests.

Decoding 2D Drivers License Barcodes

http://www.turbulence.org/Works/swipe/barcode.html

If your state driver's license has a 2d barcode on it (which is usually of the PDF417 type), you can scan or photograph the symbol and upload it to the Swipe Toolkit website shown above. You *may* or may not be able to decode the data that's contained in the barcode on your license.

Swipe's interactive map shows which data is currently encoded on U.S. state and Canadian province driver's licenses, according to usage by the website's visitors. State driver's licenses may use both 1d and 2d barcodes.

This data is often decoded by bars, convenience stores, airports and other locations when they check your identification—whether or not they inform you that they are going to scan your ID card electronically.

Appendix B – QR Code History and Specifications

How did Denso come up with the idea for QR codes?

Denso was looking for ways to put more and more information into a barcode. The first method was to "stack" barcodes, so that three barcodes, each containing different information, would be stacked to form a square, like this:

In an attempt to add even more information, Denso came up with the combination of barcode and something they called a "2d" (two-dimensional) barcode. As you can see below, there are bars on the sides and a more complex 2d code in the middle.

Denso's final version, shown below, was the one that we now use, which they named a "QR Code" for "Quick Response.". The bars are gone and the symbol consists of an information-dense matrix composed of small squares. The three large squares in the corners are placed to tell the scanner the positioning of the data modules and how the data is to be read.

How much information can a QR code contain?

The amount of information you can place into a QR code is limited. If you limit your content to numbers only, it can hold 7,089 characters. If you mix both numbers and letters, as is more commonly done, a QR code's storage capacity is limited to 4,296 characters. If you're using Kanji or Kana, you're limited to 1,817 characters—and other character-based languages are similarly limited.

If you have too much data in a QR code, it becomes very dense. Here are examples.

20 Characters   40 Characters

80 Characters   200 Characters

As you can see, depending on the finished size of your QR code, 20 to 40 characters are probably the maximum to produce an easily readable symbol. However, don't worry. That limit means almost nothing. Although the data within a QR code that can be scanned, decoded and read *without connecting to the Internet* is relatively small, you're not limited to that small amount of data. The most important use of QR codes is to *connect* your mobile phone with the Internet, and it takes very little data within the QR code to tell your phone's browser exactly where to go on the Internet. The QR code simply needs to contain the Web address for the destination website. That address can be very small, or quite long, but it will still fit within the QR code's storage ability. While standard barcodes can hold about 20 digits (perfect for ISBNs and parts numbers, for example), QR codes can hold much more information.

Note: Very long Web addresses (such as *http://www.google.com/search? q=wiki+barcodes&ie=utf-8&oe=utf-8&aq=t&client=firefox- a&rlz=1R1GGGL_en_*) can make for a more complex QR code which can be hard for mobile phone scanners to read and decode. We recommend that you use a URL shortener such as www.bit.ly to create a shorter URL which will result in a less dense QR code.

QR Code Structure

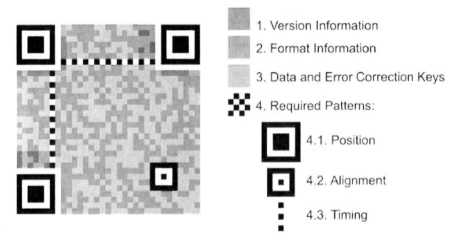

The illustration above shows the structure of a QR code. The squares in the three corners and the "dotted lines" connecting them are required and indicate the position and coordinates of the symbol in your QR code reader.

The small square near the bottom right corner is also required and indicates alignment. The remainder of the symbol contains version and format information, error correction keys, and all of the data that you encoded. Don't worry. You don't need to know any of this yourself. It's all automatically taken care of by QR code generators.

How big is a QR code?

QR codes can vary in size—and by size we mean "physical size"--the vertical and horizontal dimensions of the symbol. The symbol "version" determines how much data the symbol can hold as well as its physical dimensions.

The basic code—Version 1—is made up of 21 "modules" per side. A module is one of the black or white mini-squares that make up the QR code. So a Version 1 QR code has 21 modules on each side of the matrix, for a total of 441 modules. A Version 2 code has 25 per side. They increase by four modules per side up to Version 40, which has 177 rows and 177 columns, and can encode up to 4,296 alphanumeric characters.

The actual size of the symbol depends on the module size (the physical size of each black or white unit of data) and the symbol version (which determines the total number of modules or squares). A typical Version 2 QR code would be 12.5 mm (0.5") square, with each of its 625 modules being 0.5 mm (19.7 mils) square. Every QR code also has a four-module "quiet zone" around the outside of the symbol.

Version 4 (33 by 33 modules) is the usual maximum limit for effective scanning by mobile phones.

Why are QR codes better than regular barcodes?[5]

Large Data Content

QR codes can hold as much as several hundred times more information than a standard one-dimensional barcode. However, for ordinary use, you'll never need that much data.

Smaller Size

Because QR codes can store information vertically as well as horizontally, they can store the same amount of information in one-tenth the space of the usual barcode. (Even less with the *Micro QR Code*. See below.)

Damage Correction

QR codes have a built-in error correction capability. Data can be restored and read even if the symbol is as much as 30% obscured.

Readable from any angle

One-dimensional barcodes usually must be read with the scanner held somewhat vertical to the code. QR codes are totally omni-directional and can be scanned with the scanner held at any angle for a full 360°.

---

5   http://www.denso-wave.com/qrcode/qrfeature-e.html

Micro QR Codes

For even smaller sized codes, you can use the very small Micro QR Codes. They hold less data (a maximum of 35 numeric characters) and are designed for very small spaces, such as on printed circuit boards and other electronic parts.

You can create a Micro QR Code at no charge at:

> http://keremerkan.net/qr-code-and-2d-code-generator/

Appendix C – Entering Text into QR Code Generators

With most QR code generators, it's very simple to fill out the form for the code's content. The site will display very clearly on your screen exactly what you need to enter, and any technical language such as "http://" will be built-in.

However, just so you know, and in case you need them sometime, here are full instructions.

URLs
A URL is a Universal Resource Locator, a fancy—but the original and official—name for a web address.

As Google says with its Zxing project:

> The most common application of barcodes is to encode the text of URLs, such as http://google.com/m. To do so, simply encode exactly the text of the URL in the barcode: "http://google.com/m". Include the protocol ("http://") to ensure it is recognized as a URL.

> Most QR code generators will have the "http://" command built in.

Google also notes that sometimes QR codes can work better if you use all uppercase letters when you enter the text for URLs. Experiment to see how it works for your addresses.

E-mail Addresses
It's best to use the standard web mail command: mailto:mick@westsong.com. The "mailto:" makes it absolutely clear to your decoder what's intended. Most QR code generators will have the "mailto" command built in.

Telephone Numbers
To make it clear to a phone barcode reader, use "tel:" before the number, although most QR code generators will have "tel:" built in.

Use international prefixes so that people from other countries can easily access the phone number. For example, to use the US phone number 212-555-1212, you should type "tel:+12125551212". The "+1" prefix is the country code for the U.S. and will make it usable outside the United States, as well as within.

Contact Information

The QR code generator that you are using will provide specific lines such as name, address, phone and email so you will know exactly what it is capable of encoding.

SMS

An SMS is a short alphanumeric message of no more than 140 characters. SMS means "Short Message Service" and SMS is commonly known as "texting".

To enter an SMS shortcode, use the command "sms:" at the beginning. Example: sms:12345. Most QR code generators will have the "sms:" built in, either visibly or behind-the-scenes.

Geographic Information

A QR code can contain geographic information, such as the latitude, longitude and even altitude of a point on earth. For example, to encode Google's New York office location, which is at 40.71872 degrees N latitude, 73.98905 degrees W longitude, at a point 100 meters above sea level, one would encode "geo:40.71872,-73.98905,100".

Appendix D - Not Barcodes, but Kind of Similar

Location-Based Applications

As you're driving or walking through town, your phone rings and says "Don't forget you wanted to buy some towel hangers for the kitchen. You're near a hardware store." Or "The police department reports that there have been recent car thefts in this area. Make sure your car is parked in a well-lighted place and locked." Or how about "You're two minutes away from the coffee house and it's having a special sale on your favorite dark-roasted Panamanian blend." Or "There's a reported heavy rain storm due here in the next 15 minutes. You might want to go inside one of these nearby cafes to wait it out." All of this is possible with Location Based Service.

Location Based Service (LBS)-enabled mobile phones use their GPS (Global Positioning System) capability to tell you where you are, who and what is near you, and what the conditions are now and in the future, such as weather, traffic or planned events. They can give you navigation directions, whether you're on foot, on bike, in your car, or taking public transportation, as well as information on nearby friends, businesses, and conditions.

Using your LBS-equipped phone, you can send or receive messages based on your location. Since your phone, using GPS, knows where you are, it can provide information such as the following.

- "Where's the nearest Thai restaurant?" - Phone displays names, locations, reviews, and even coupons.

- If you've enabled Sales Alerts, as you walk along city streets, the phone can let you know which shops—of the type of business, or brand name, which you previously specified—have sale prices on the type of product you're interested in.

- If you've enabled Traffic Alerts, your phone can let you know that there is congestion or an accident ahead, and recommend an alternative route.

- If you've enabled Nearby Friends, you can be notified when friends are within a certain distance.

- If you've enabled Location Settings, when you're at your office your phone can automatically use a specified ringtone at a specified volume when your phone "rings"—and a different configuration when you're at home.

- If you prefer having your coffee every morning at a certain time and you're in a new city, it will automatically notify you at that time where the locations are of the nearest coffee houses.

- If you've enabled Virtual Tagging you'll be notified when you pass a spot where there is a Virtual Tag of likely interest to you. The tag may also allow you to add your comments to those of previous viewers.

Augmented Reality

Augmented Reality (AR), also called *Virtual Tagging*,

- Combines the "real" physical world with the "virtual" digital/online world

- Takes place in real time and can be interactive

Commonly known examples of AR are the yellow "first down" lines seen in television broadcasts of American football games, and the colored trail showing location and direction of the puck in TV broadcasts of ice hockey games. The real-world elements are the football field and players, and the virtual element is the yellow line, which is drawn over the image by computers in real time. Similarly, rugby fields and cricket pitches are branded by their sponsors using Augmented Reality; giant logos are inserted onto the fields when viewed on television.

In some cases, the modification of reality goes beyond mere augmentation. For example, advertisements may be blocked out (partially or wholly diminished) and replaced with different advertisements. Such ad replacement is an example of Mediated reality, a more general concept than AR.

Television telecasts of swimming events also often have a virtual line which indicates the position of the current world record holder at that time.

In some current applications like in cars or airplanes, this is usually a head-up display integrated into the windshield. - *Wikipedia*

Augmented Reality/Virtual Tagging in the mobile world does not involve television, or anything such as airplane head-up displays. Neither does it involve QR codes or any type of barcode. In fact it doesn't involve anything physical.

A virtual tag is "virtually" created when you use a virtual tagging application at a location. The LBS (Location Based Service) feature on your smart phone will determine the geographical coordinates of your location: your precise latitude and longitude. You can leave a virtual "tag" at this location. The tag is stored in a database according to its geographical coordinates. This virtual tag can be text, audio, photos, or video—or a link to a website.

When someone comes to, or close to, this location and has the same application on their phone, the virtual tag that you created will be visible on their phone.

There are a number of mobile phone applications that can create and read virtual tags, but there is as yet no standard for these tags. This means that a particular application can read only those virtual tags placed by someone else with the *same* application. It's likely that over time one or two methods of creating and storing virtual tags will become standard, just as QR codes have become a standard for 2d barcodes.

To find augmented reality applications for your phone, go to your phone's application store and search for "augmented reality".

Virtual Graffiti

Virtual Graffiti is a form of virtual tagging and consists mainly of virtual objects and/or digital messages, images, multimedia or other annotations or graphics applied to public locations, landmarks or surfaces such as walls, train stations, bridges, etc.

Virtual Graffiti applications use virtual reality (AR) and ubiquitous [everywhere] computing to anchor Virtual Graffiti to physical landmarks or objects in the real world. The virtual content is then viewable through devices such as personal computers, set-top boxes or mobile handsets, such as mobile phones or tablets. The virtual world provides content, graphics, and applications to the user that are not available in the real world. Virtual Graffiti is a novel initiative aimed at delivering messaging and social multimedia content to mobile applications and devices based on the location, identity, and community of the participating entity. - *Wikipedia*

Virtual Pollution / Virtual Littering

Currently, the lack of standards for virtually tagging has one major advantage. It's true that the lack of a standard means that you can use a specific application to read only the tags created by someone using that same application. The upside is that at popular locations you do not have to see countless tags created by a multitude of *other* applications.

It's quite probable that once a standard is developed, or at least applications are created that can read a large number of different proprietary virtual tags (just as many barcode readers can now read a number of different types of both 1d and 2d barcodes), those popular locations will be subject to Virtual Littering or Virtual Pollution. It will be a Tragedy of the Virtual Commons.

This potential mass virtual pollution will have to be dealt with, probably with some sort of filtering system in which the mobile user can specify the characteristics of the virtual tags she wishes to "see".

Internet of Things

Although it doesn't involved QR codes, there is growing interest in an "Internet of Things". This simply means that more and more electrical and electronic gadgets and appliances that we usually take for granted will be hooked up to the Internet, usually through a WiFi connection.

For example, you could use your mobile phone to turn on your Digital Video Recorder, or to start pre-heating your oven. You might want to turn the heat on in your home, or check to see that you turned all the lights out when you left. Perhaps you might want to see if there's still some of your favorite beverage in the vending machine down the hall (actually this was a *very* early use of the Internet). Or you might want to look at a webcam that shows how the babysitter and your child are doing (a very frequent use these days).

More unusual, perhaps, you could monitor the water saturation level of your garden's soil, and if too low, turn on your drip irrigation system for a while. (Even better, your garden could decide *itself* that its soil was getting dry and either start watering itself or check with you for your permission.) While this wouldn't require use of QR codes, the Internet of Things is another one of the remarkable ways you can benefit when you connect with the Internet through your mobile phone.

Here's what Wikipedia says about the Internet of Things. The focus here is on embedding or attaching an RFID (Radio Frequency Identification Device) on every object, but QR codes can serve the same purpose in many cases, and at no cost.

> In computing, the Internet of Things refers to a network of objects, such as household appliances...The idea is as simple as its application is difficult. If all cans, books, shoes or parts of cars are equipped with minuscule identifying devices, daily life on our planet will undergo a

transformation. Things like running out of stock or wasted products will no longer exist as we will know exactly what is being consumed on the other side of the globe. Theft will be a thing of the past as we will know where a product is at all times. The same applies to parcels lost in the post.

If all objects of daily life, from yoghurt to an airplane, are equipped with radio tags, they can be identified and managed by computers in the same way humans can. The system would therefore be able to instantaneously identify any kind of object.

The Internet of objects should encode 50 to 100 trillion objects and follow the movement of those objects. Every human being is surrounded by 1,000 to 5,000 objects. - *Wikipedia*

Appendix E – Academic Research

There is a growing body of literature in the academic world on the use of QR codes. For academics, university students and interested parties at all levels of education who are researching this topic, here are some useful websites and an annotated bibliography.

Andy Ramsden, Head of e-Learning at the University of Bath

Dr. Ramsden has done extensive research on e-learning and the use of QR codes. We recommend both his blog and the following working paper.

Blog

QR Codes at Bath - http://blogs.bath.ac.uk/qrcode/

Paper

Ramsden, A., 2008. *The use of QR codes in Education: A getting started guide for academics.* Working Paper. University of Bath .

http://opus.bath.ac.uk/11408/

This document is part of a series of reports which make up a scoping study on the potential of using QR codes in learning and teaching which was commissioned by the JISC. The document is intended as an introduction to the role of QR codes in education. In particular, it starts to find answers to the following key questions: What are QR codes? How might they be used in education? How do I create my own QR codes? Can students engage with this technology? Where on the web might I find up to date information about QR codes being used in education?

Arnall, T., "Physical hyperlinks", *New York City Mobile Camp*, 19 May 2007, New York, NY, USA. at http://www.nearfield.org/downloads/MCNYCPhysicalHyperlinks.pdf on 22 March 2010.

The author asks a significant question: "In evaluating these ideas we have to ask, are they better than a simple poster or other visual information like signage?" The use of QR codes in this project must provide an experience not available in any other way. Arnall mentions one particularly intriguing use of QR codes: At certain locations in a town, a student placed posters that contained some text and a barcode that led to a website with a newspaper article about an event that had happened at that same location.

Ceipidor, U., Medaglia, C., Perrone, A. De Marsico, M, and Di Romano, G., "A museum mobile game for children using QR codes", Interaction Design and Children, *Proceedings of the 8th International Conference on Interaction Design and Children,* 2009, Como, Italy, pp. 282-283. At http://portal.acm.org.ezproxy.brighton.ac.uk/citation.cfm?id=1551857 on 16 March 2010.

Proposes the use of QR codes to create a treasure hunt for children within a museum. Children scan QR codes with their camera phones to get riddles and clues to answers. Success at each location provides a clue to the next location. At the end, successful students are given a reward souvenir. Although aimed at 11-14 year olds, the concept could work with any age, and could be a useful community-wide activity to increase public awareness of QR codes.

Epstein, M. and Vergani, S., "History unwired:Mobile narrative in historic cities", *Proceedings of the working conference on advanced visual interfaces,* AVI 2006, 23-26 May 2006, Venezia, Italy, ACM Press, 2006. pp.302-305, http://portal.acm.org.ezproxy.brighton.ac.uk/citation.cfm?doid=1133265.1133327

History Unwired investigates the narrative uses of mobile technology in historic cities. This paper focuses on a particular neighborhood in Venice. As the paper states "the project comes at a time in which the number of visitors in Venice is rapidly increasing and tourists are spending less time in the city." One goal of the project was to attract visitors to areas of Venice other than the immediate city center. All information was on a handheld device, provided to each visitor involved in the test. Although the content and path of the walk were pre-programmed, the project's presentation of content can be useful in other circumstances. For example, a building that was "off limits" could still be seen virtually as visitors watched, from outside the building, an audio video tour of the inside of the building on their handheld device. An interesting way to integrate local businesses into the tour was a stroll down the "Paved Canal of the Baker", which led naturally to the last remaining bakery, where the visual and audio experiences of the visitors were reinforced by another sensory input: smell. (See http://web.mit.edu/frontiers for an interactive view of the project and the tour.)

Fielding, A. "Cyber space, meat space and a sense of place: Lessons from the interplay of the online and offline worlds", Walk21.com, *website,* London, UK, at http://walk21.com/paper_search/results_detail.asp?Paper=441 accessed 19 March 2010.

Covers such topics as walking directions, modeling of real spaces (such as Second Life), organizing of subversion of public space, pervasive gaming, location-based activities, use of GPS to encourage walking, and location identification. An excellent overview of the current state of cyberspace trends and an enjoyable pointer to possibilities for this project, particularly for encouraging people to walk in public spaces.

Haisler, D. "White paper: Redefining government communication with QR-codes", *City of Manor,* Texas, September 2009, at www.cityofmanor.org/comwhitepaper.pdf on 16 March 2010.

Produced by the Chief Information Officer of Manor, Texas, this paper discusses the planning, deployment, benefits and results of a campaign in that town to assist citizen communication, emergency management, and information on historical sites. Includes photographs of various versions of signs and their placement at locations throughout town, as well as tips on campaign marketing and the recommended amount of text in a QR code.

Hill, N., "Hyperlinking reality", *Library Journal,* July 2009, p38-39., at http://www.libraryjournal.com/article/CA6668443.html on 22 March 2010.

Article by a public librarian on the growing use of QR codes in public and university libraries. Codes are being used to obtain call numbers for individual books as well as for access to the full online catalog. Discusses the value of QR codes for social media, so that a QR code can connect not just to a static image or article but to an active website such as a blog, producing "dynamic graffiti" that enables many people to take part virtually in a location-linked discussion. In one sense, entire discussions can be considered to "inhabit" a single QR code. The code is not just a link but an open portal into a virtual world, or as Hill calls it "a mirror of a specific location in the real world". The concept of linking to an active website may be incorporated into this project.

Inscho, J. ,"Do-it-yourself QR codes: A 4-step guide", *Mattress Factory:* Art you can get into, blog post, 10 September 2009, at http://artyoucangetinto.blogspot.com/2009/09/do-it-yourself-qr-codes-4-step-guide.html on 21 March 2010.

Apparently written by a staff member of the Mattress Factory, a museum of contemporary art in Pittsburgh, Pennsylvania, USA. This blog is a practical guide to the use of QR codes in a museum, gallery or other indoor space. Designed to help other museums create similar systems without the cost of using outside consultants. Tips include optimal physical size of QR codes for viewing and scanning, and the blog's comments section offers very interesting viewpoints.

Jacks, B., "Reimagining walking: Four practices", *Journal of Architectural Education*, 2004, Vol. 57 (3), pp.5-9,

The abstract for Jacks' paper says: "The simple act of walking has been rendered alien and almost obsolete in the contemporary landscape...Ordinary walking has become a rebellious and subversive act." The paper concludes with: "The practices of walking—modest and ordinary, rebellious and subversive—offer a grounding and a path in which beauty and social goals are united." Paradoxically, through the use of QR codes, the technology that has helped contribute to our lack of walking can help restore our interest, enjoyment, and desire to walk, particularly throughout our community.

Koskinen, I. And Battarbee, K., "Thinking about sound in mobile multimedia", Workshop on Pervasive Image Capture and Sharing · *Ubicomp 2006*, 18 September 2006, Berkeley, CA, USA. At http://groups.ischool.berkeley.edu/pics/papers/Koskinen_Battarbee_sound_in_mm_pics06.pdf on 22 March 2010.

This paper proposes that sound does not have to be synchronized to images to be effective in mobile multimedia. While the focus is on social media—primarily multimedia messages between people—the concept is applicable to sound and images retrieved through the use of QR codes.

Long Beach Peninsula Visitors Bureau, "Long Beach, Washington is first in the Northwest to use QR codes to target visitors at points of interest", *press release*, 10 March 1020, at http://funbeach.com/qrpress/first-in-northwest on 14 March 2010.

Press release announcing the launch of a project in the tourist town of Long Beach, Washington that uses QR codes at 29 different locations to provide smartphone-equipped visitors with location-specific text information. The project includes a self-guided tour of an 8.5-mile long paved, coastal interpretive path. Future plans call for linking to video clips, audio recordings, and slide shows. The Long Beach project serves as a useful and encouraging example to this project.

Ljungstrand, P. and Holmquist, L.E., "Webstickers: Using physical objects as WWW bookmarks" *PLAY: Applied research on art and technology*, Viktoria Institute, Gothenburg, Sweden: at http://www.viktoria.se/ubicomp/webstickers.pdf on 18 March 2010.

The proposed system uses pre-printed barcodes to associate URLs with physical objects. The object itself becomes, in effect, a three-dimensional bookmark for a website, a bookmark that will exist as long as the object does. Although the system was designed with standard barcodes, it would function more efficiently with QR codes. Barcodes require an intermediary server for analysis, whereas QR codes can contain more extensive information and point directly to a webpage.

[Murmur] Toronto, website, at www.murmurtoronto.ca on 22 March 2010.

[Murmur] is an oral history project that records stories and memories told about specific geographic locations. A visitor (or new neighbor) can go to designated points in a neighborhood and listen to the voice of knowledgeable neighbors relating their memories about each spot and its significance to them. The program started in Toronto, Ontario, Canada and has spread to a number of other countries (For example, see www.murmurgeelong.com). Initially the program placed actual phones at the locations. Currently they are providing phone numbers, which visitors can dial from their own personal phones. The advantage of phone numbers is that the user does not need an Internet-enabled/barcode reading phone. The disadvantage is that the user has to dial a number, and the retrieved information can only be audio. QR codes are probably next; perhaps starting with this project.

O'Hara, K., Kindberg, T., Glancy, M., Baptista, L. and Sukumaran, B., "Social practices in location-based collecting", Proceedings of the SIGCHI conference on Human factors in computing systems, *Conference on Human Factors in Computing Systems*, San Jose, California, USA 2007, pp. 1225-1234.

This paper discusses not the *acquisition* of content through the use of mobile phones but the collection and retention of that content. It suggests that the content can continue to have value, even *increasing* value, after the user has left the original location. The study was conducted at London Zoo. Students nine to twelve years old were given their own personal webpage which they would "fill" with content acquired as they walked throughout the zoo with mobile camera phones provided by the researchers. After their zoo experience, the children were able to access their own personal zoo webpage from their schools and homes, where they could show families and friends their "collection" of virtual souvenirs. Although this project was conducted with provided phones, it could also be done with visitors' own personal phones. The most important feature of this paper is the emphasis on collecting and retaining content acquired on a tour, which may be possible to test within this project's time frame.

Paay, J., and Kjeldskov, J. with Christensen, A., Ibsen, A., Jensen, D., Nielsen, G. and Vutborg, R. "Location-based storytelling in the urban environment", 2008, OZCHI, Vol. 287, pp.122-129, *Proceedings of the 20th*

Australasian Conference on Computer-Human Interaction: Designing for Habitus and Habitat, Cairns, Australia.

This paper reports on an organized game in which participants used mobile phones and headsets to hear a carefully planned and orchestrated narrative using video, audio and images. Most importantly for this project, it opens up the concept of using audio fiction—perhaps mini-playlets—to make locations come alive to visitors, integrating real facts and physical characteristics of the site into an informational narrative.

Turismo Torino e Provincia, "Technology for tourists from the new interactive destination website www.turismotorino.org to microsoft tag technology!", press release, 12 March 2010, Torino, Italy, at http://www.turismotorino.org/pdf/Press_release.pdf on 16 March 2010.

Announcement by the Turin Tourist Board that Turin has become the first "colour tagged" city in the world. The tourism office will, at no charge, install the Microsoft Tag reader on visitors' phones (or they can download it prior to their visit). Colored tiles on the ground in front of various tourist attractions in the city will contain Microsoft "tags", similar in some ways to QR codes. Visitor will receive information in text, video or audio format, or even gain access to reserved areas. While this action in Turin is beneficial for the expansion of the concept of using mobile phones to access tourist information, their use of Microsoft tags, which though colorful are proprietary, further complicates the technology by requiring an intermediary link through Microsoft servers before accessing the website containing the desired information, thus leading away from the ubiquitous adoption of QR codes.

Index

Alphabetical Index

A to Z of QR Codes

Making QR codes

Visit Us Online

www.scanmebook.com

CPSIA information can be obtained at www.ICGtesting.com
Printed in the USA
BVOW02s1600111015

421358BV00005B/154/P